My Mother's Soldier

Mary Elizabeth Bailey

TRILOGY CHRISTIAN PUBLISHERS
TUSTIN, CA

Trilogy Christian Publishers
A Wholly Owned Subsidiary of Trinity Broadcasting Network
2442 Michelle Drive
Tustin, CA 92780

For information, address Trilogy Christian Publishing
Rights Department, 2442 Michelle Drive, Tustin, Ca 92780.

Trilogy Christian Publishing/ TBN and colophon are trademarks of Trinity Broadcasting Network.

For information about special discounts for bulk purchases, please contact Trilogy Christian Publishing.

Manufactured in the United States of America

10 9 8 7 6 5 4 3 2 1

Library of Congress Cataloging-in-Publication Data is available.

ISBN 978-1-64773-208-0

ISBN 978-1-64773-209-7

Contents

Dedication

I write this book for the little girl who needed healing and most importantly needed to forgive herself. This can be a very difficult process, but an intimate relationship with God (papa) is a must. There were and still are days that the struggle is real. The memories are raw and feel like this tragedy happened only moments ago...we are numbly caught in a time warp. Our heart raced, our vision blurred...but at that moment we fall to our knees and ask "papa" to take this burden because it is then we realize it is too heavy to carry alone.

I dedicate this journey, this book to each and every person facing challenges, heartache, and disappointments. To that person who is ready to give up, instead, I encourage you to rise up. Rise up and face the challenge. Find the David inside of you and take down the Goliath that is standing over you.

To the many children who find themselves in foster care. The fear of the unknown is scary. The emotions, tears, sadness, and the loss of the life you knew. I ask you to embrace those moments, dig deeper than you ever thought possible. This isn't your fault; it may feel like it, but believe me when I tell you it is not your fault. I know you miss your mother and your father. It is innate in us to want to protect the only thing we know, and even through abuse and neglect we still seek to protect the very ones who inflict such pain. But remember this can be an opportunity for a new beginning.

For my brother(s) and sister, I am sorry for the heartache and pain. I only hope you find forgiveness in your hearts and let go of the past. Recreate a better life and future not only for yourself but for your children. Break the cycle...break the chains and be free. To the youngest brother, I loved you dearly; I am and always will be heartbroken that your life was cut short. I know you're free and well.

Lastly, I dedicate this book to my sweet loving Grandmother. My love for you will live forever – though you did not. A part of me will always be missing until I see you again. I am sorry I wasn't there the day you left this earth. But you took a piece of me with you, and you left some of you here with me. I have only one picture of you and me together. I cherish this more than you know. Remember the pennies I played with and you hid for me to find. I'm still finding them – at the most needed times you show up. Sometimes the penny is well-worn and I can barely see a date on it. Sometimes it's fresh and new. I know what you're saying to me every time I find one of these "pennies from heaven." I hope you know how much you meant to me while here on this earth. I never really got to thank you for all you did to make life tolerable. After all, I was only 13 when you passed away. It is a day and a phone call I will never forget. You remembered me in your final days when dementia had taken all your memory of your children and life...still you ask about that little red-headed girl. She is here, you are there, and your memories are present within me.

Acknowledgements

I would like to thank the Department of Health and Human Services for taking care of me and helping me with the transition into foster care. A special thanks to Jean Bulka and Jim Webber.

I want to thank the judge that presided over the trial. Your compassion and care for me was evident from day one. You made me feel comfortable in undoubtedly one of the worst situations I could have found myself. You listened to me, you allowed me to feel as though I had a voice. For that I thank you.

Thank you to each and every one of my foster care families, as well as my respite families. Your love and support made me the person I am today. I was fortunate enough to get a little piece of all of you. It's like the song by Dolly Parton "Coat of many colors" I was loved and cared for. Thank you so much.

Thank you to the Guardian Ad Litem's/CASA though I did not have the privilege of having someone such as this when I was in foster care. I see and view it as a wonderful privilege. I encourage anyone who has the time and wants to help and be a voice for these children to step up and volunteer. To all the many wonderful individuals, who do this day in and day out, Thank you. You are like angels to these children, and we can't thank you enough.

I want to thank my teachers and my coaches. Many of you were good to me and understood my challenges. Some of you did not. That's ok. For those individuals I choose forgiveness.

Calvin Sumner my childhood therapist. Thank you. You are a remarkable man; you helped me through some of those most difficult times in my life as a child. You pushed me to face my demons when I wanted to hide them away. You were patient and understanding. You encouraged me to cry, to talk, but most importantly you allowed me to be silent when there were no words... only pain. I will forever be grateful.

To my Pastor and his wife at Rock Cave Baptist Church in West Virginia. Thank you for taking the time to love me, and most importantly thank you for introducing me to God. This is the greatest of all gifts.

To a dear gentleman who entered my life, and read my story. Though your time with me was short it was powerful. I believe people enter our lives for many reasons and sometimes in this case for only a season. They come and go – but can leave a lasting impact on you. Your encouragement and belief in me were what I needed at the time to get where I am today. Thank you... and thank you for the pink ball...I will forever cherish that gift. It will always be a reminder to never look back.

My dear friends who know my story and who love and encourage me daily. Who see beyond the scars and love and cherish the women I am inside and out. Your kindness, the moments you cried with me, prayed for me, stood by me and encouraged me. You have no idea what that means.

My publishing company Trilogy Christian Publishing (a subsidiary of TBN) after many attempts and rejections at publishing, you saw a story that needed to be told. Thank you for believing in me. I pray we can change lives through this book. If we can save one, that's one less tragedy in this cruel world.

Lastly and most importantly, I want to thank with every fiber of my being my heavenly Father. God, who would I be today without you? Where would I be? In my darkest days, you sat with me. You knew my needs with every tear that fell from my eyes. You knew my heart when I couldn't find the words to speak. You knew me before I was ever born while I was in the womb you formed me. Your promised in Jeremiah 29:11 (NIV) "For I know the plans I have for you declares the LORD, plans to prosper you and not harm you, plans to give you hope and a future" You have done that and more. If I never received another single blessing I could leave this world a blessed and thankful soul. Your love for me has been remarkable and I have felt you with me all along my journey. Sometimes...many times actually. I have taken the wrong path, but even when I do your always ahead of me putting me back on the right path. You have never left me. Thank you, papa, thank you.

Preface

The book *My Mother's Soldier* was written with great apprehension and emotional turmoil. My suppressed childhood memories were certain to reemerge, and the pain that accompanied the memories I loathed. I knew that writing this book would force me to face my devastating past and relive memories that I had buried deep within myself. This is the story of my childhood. A childhood filled with physical, mental, and emotional abuse that I suffered at the hands of my mother and step-father. A childhood that would eventually lead to child-exploitation beyond one's comprehension. Many of the facts that are revealed in this book were unknown to me until I viewed the video footage of my mother's murder trial. I was given the videotapes when I was sixteen years old, but the tapes would sit dormant in a small hope-chest for the next sixteen years of my life; never to be viewed by me or anyone else. Much of this book was written from information that came out during the trial, under sworn testimony, as well as my personal childhood memories.

As an adult, I realized that my story is not unique to just me. Many children suffer from child abuse and neglect around the world. Like me, many of them find themselves trapped in the foster-care system leading to a life of uncertainty, just as I did. Helping others to overcome adversity and realize that they are not alone is my ultimate goal. My life has been difficult, but put-ting faith in God allowed me the opportunity to thrive, as well as the will-power to survive. This is a powerful and inspiring story that will bewilder readers and leave them searching their hearts and minds for understanding, as well as a renewed faith in hope and determination. My hope is that my story will give readers the faith and courage to rise above the turmoil that infiltrates their lives and move forward with their lives regardless of their circumstances. If telling my story to the world inspires just one person to maintain hope and faith, then the pain and suffering associated with revealing my past will have been a rewarding endeavor.

While this book *My Mother's Soldier* encompasses my story of childhood abuse and neglect, the book also de-tails the part of my tragic childhood that I share with so many foster children such as adult-life without parents, family, or a place to call home. The child abuse and neglect I experienced as a young child I have managed to overcome; however, the struggles of life without a family have been my biggest challenge. I have found peace and solace in this area since writing this book. Through my journey, I have reconnected with a few people that loved me when I was a child, and still love me to this day.

As you read the text that lies ahead, you will feel sorrow for what a young child had to endure as her journey comes full circle. You will possibly even relive some of your own trials. This book was written to help others deal with some of the challenges we all face during our existence here on this earth.

Hope & Healing

"Mary, wake up I want to talk to you about something." Early on the morning of February 24, 1987, my mother woke me from a light sleep. What she wanted to talk to me about would forever change my life by leaving me without family or a feeling of belonging for many years to come. This is the story of my childhood without parents to guide me and a life without a family. It is also the story of a mother who sentenced me to a lifetime of nightmares and memories that no child should have to endure. These memories include child abuse, poverty, neglect, violence, and ultimately murder.

More than thirty-three years have passed since this terrible tragedy in my life. Although I have concealed the scars and moved through life as though nothing ever happened, I realized as I grew older how important it was to face my dysfunctional childhood and the fallout from events that transpired when I was only eleven years old. Until recently, I have never spoken openly of the devastating events that will come to life in this book.

For many years shame has kept me from expressing my feelings about my childhood to friends, and family. When I am compelled to recount some of the events of my young life, I often ask those with whom I am talking what they consider the worst thing that a child could be subject to in an abusive situation. Their guesses never even come close. When I tell them my story, they are amazed and shocked. Most say that it's more than their minds can comprehend. I have decided to go public with my story for two very different reasons. The first reason is personal healing. I need to get this story out in the open so that I can quit running from my past. Feeling as though I were living a lie, and suppressing the ugly truth about my past has taken a toll on me as a person. At times I felt that I had been living in the Witness Protection Program, never divulging anything about what made me the person I am today. Secondly, helping others. Although my tragic story is unlike most, children all over the world are struggling not only with abusive parents but also with the foster-care system. While my time in foster care was better than abuse and neglect at the hands of my mother and stepfather, my experience as a foster child continues to haunt me as an adult. Much of the pain I suffered during childhood came after the horrific events of February 1987. Imagine for a moment being removed from your home without any notice and taken to a strange town with no suitcase, toothbrush, or clothes. People you have never met before greet you at the door of their house, while the person who brought you there drives away. You can't call home, and even if you could no one would answer the phone. Everyone you know seems to have disappeared from the face of the earth. When nightfall comes, you are given a small cot in a room with two people you have never met.

Welcome to the foster-care system in America. I lived under this regimen from the time I was eleven years old until I graduated from high school at age seventeen. Don't get me wrong. I am forever grateful for the care I received from each of my foster families, of which there were three, along with a few "respite" families that stepped-in to care for me when the foster family I was living with wanted time to vacation alone with their own children. However, I left the foster-care system at seventeen with no real sense of family. In fact, my senior yearbook's family page was left blank because I had no family to write about. Although I was provided for as a foster child, there has to be a way to turn a scared child into someone who feels that she or he belongs in the world.

It takes work to make this happen, and I am dedicated to making a difference. I don't want any child to grow up feeling bereft of someone to call Mom or Dad, or at least a place to call "home" after becoming an adult. Foster children deserve to have someone with who to share life's ups and downs. So many times I have needed the advice that only a parent can give. Never having known my biological father, who is now deceased, I always wondered what it would be like to be "Daddy's little girl". I also wondered what it would be like to go shopping with my mother or just have lunch together. Now that I am older you might think those desires have faded, but in fact they have intensified. Though I am proud of everything I have accomplished in life thus far, I long still for the love of a family. One of my goals is to inform current and potential foster parents about is-sues foster children must cope with and to push for additional training for foster parents across the country. I also hope to establish a home for foster children where they can make the transition prior to being placed with a foster family. Foster care will always be needed, and most of the time foster care is better than the other option—a life of abuse and neglect.

As I reflect back on my life before foster care, I realize what a hopeless situation I was in, trapped in a life of despair with little hope of escape. My abusive step-father cared nothing for me, and my neglectful mother should never have had children. Then there was my sweet grandmother, who deeply loved me but who was simply too old and too fragile to stop the abuse. The only hope I found as a ten-year-old child was a Baptist preacher named Jim McCall who picked me up in his white pickup truck every Sunday and Wednesday and took me to his church. Although this was only a temporary escape from the madness, I was so happy to be safe from the abuse and in loving hands if just for a few hours. I learned a lot about prayer and love in my time with Jim and his wife Kay. I also came to realize that there had to be a better way of life for me. Very early on I knew that somehow I must find a way to overcome adversity. Now thirty-three years old, I have made great strides in healing. While I still face daily challenges relating to my childhood, I have found ways to rise above them. As a result of my horrific past, I set some pretty high standards for myself as an adult. I would not live in poverty as I did as a child, I would not fall victim to an abusive man as my mother did, and I would not be a drain on society.

Thousands of foster children across the country fail miserably as adults. Statistics show that 80 percent of them end up imprisoned or homeless. I was one of the fortunate ones who made it, which I attribute to faith and determination rather than luck. In fact, luck had absolutely nothing to do with my decision that I would build a better life for myself. After my foster parents dropped me off at Marshall University when I was seventeen years old, I quickly came to realize that if I was going to make it, I would have to do so on my own. I again found myself in uncharted waters more than one hundred fifty miles from my hometown with no car and very little money. Thankfully, I had a full scholarship and a dorm room. An absence of parental guidance resulted in making plenty of mistakes as a young adult, but I was determined never to return to the lifestyle I knew as a young child.

What would have become of me if I had not been forced into the foster care system? How many more times would I have had to move as a young child? How much more abuse would I have had to endure at the hands of my stepfather? Would I ever have made it through high school? Would I have gotten involved with drugs and sex at an early age as my mother did? While the events of February 1987 were tragic for many people, these were the challenges I would have faced had things not transpired as they did. Because my early childhood was far from normal, we should start from the very beginning.

CHAPTER 2

Better Days

I had to move nine times during the first ten years of my life. Consequently, my early years are a bit of a blur. In fact, I really had no idea of all the places I lived until I started writing this book and drew a timeline to pinpoint the locations, years, and memories of where I lived as a child. I was overwhelmed to find that I had moved an astonishing nine times between 1981 and 1986. Given all these moves, it is a miracle I made it through elementary school. You also should understand that nearly all the communities mentioned in this book were within twenty to thirty miles of one another. The place where I experienced the most stability as a child was in Lawford, West Virginia, where I lived from birth until five years of age.

I was born in the early morning hours of October 25, 1975 in Grantsville, West Virginia, to a young un-wed mother. My biological mother, to whom I will be referring to as Veronica throughout this book, was only seventeen when I was born. Veronica was an inconsistent mother figure, to say the least. She lived with her parents in the small mountain community of Lawford when I was born, and she was rarely present during my infant years as well as my young childhood. She preferred going out with friends and partying instead of being a dedicated mother to her infant daughter. After all, she was but a child herself. She didn't even know she was pregnant with me until she was well into her third trimester. Her mother became alarmed when she learned that Veronica had not had a menstrual period in more than five months. So off to the doctor they went to discover that she was six months pregnant at the young age of sixteen. Although Veronica would call on the father of the unborn child for support, her calls went unanswered.

My biological father was unknown to me throughout my entire childhood, and I met him only once after I had reached adulthood. The only real parental figures I had in my life were Veronica's parents, my grandfather Houston Butler, and my grandmother Ella Butler. I lived in Lawford with my grandparents from the time I was born until I was five years old. Though they were deeply poverty-stricken, I had the opportunity to be loved by these two wonderful people. My grandparents gave me a sense of family, something I would lose in the years to come. We lived in a small shingle-sided house that had three bedrooms, one bathroom, a living room, and a kitchen with an old gas stove. An enormous oak tree situated in the back yard was my favorite place to play during hot summer days. The big oak cast a shadow over the house in the afternoon, allowing the temperature inside to be tolerable in the evening hours. Winters, however, were vicious in the mountains of West Virginia. I remember the cold winds ripping up the hollow, making a howling noise as they moved through the attic. It was so cold in the winter months that my grandfather covered all the windows with clear plastic to keep the mountain air from seeping through the drafty casements.

My grandfather, Houston Butler, was born on February 3, 1908. He was sixty-seven years old when I came into the world. He was a tall, medium built man who always wore blue Dickie's and matching long-sleeved shirts. I can't recall a time when he wore anything else. A retired coal miner who had worked hard over the years to provide for his family, he suffered from an irreversible lung disease caused by breathing in too much coal dust in the mines. Some of my first memories of my grandfather are of the two of us sitting under the big oak tree in the back yard. He would sharpen his pocket knife on a well-worn flint while

I admired his precise motion as he stroked the blade across the stone.

After spending what seemed like an eternity sharpening his "Old Timer" pocket knife, he would send me off to the edge of the woods to find a good whittle stick. He didn't want just any stick. He wanted one of just the right diameter and length. He even had moisture criteria that I had to consider when looking for the perfect whittle stick. "Not too wet, not too dry," he would say. When I returned with a stick, he would always say, "That one is just right, Princess." Sadly, my grandfather eventually succumbed to black lung disease in 1981. While my grandfather gave me lots of love and attention, my grandmother stole my heart with her kindness and generosity.

My grandmother, Ella Butler, was a sweet and caring lady who always made sure I knew how much she loved me. She was born in 1911 and grew up as a coal miner's daughter. She and my grandfather had five children, the youngest being my mother Veronica. One of their children, a daughter named Ruthie Mae Butler, was killed at the age of five when she was struck by a car while crossing the road to check the mailbox. Not long after Ruthie Mae's death, my grandmother became pregnant with Veronica. She was forty-eight when she gave birth to her. They had such a soft spot for little girls that they could hardly bring themselves to discipline Veronica. If I were to be spoiled in any way during my childhood, my grandma would be the one to do it.

My grandmother never let a day pass without telling me how much she loved me. She gave me lots of hugs and always bought me a little sack of pink mint candy when we went to the country store. I also can still remember waking up every morning to the aroma of coffee brewing in the kitchen. My granny loved coffee. There would always be a big blue can of Maxwell House sitting on the countertop. She made the best country breakfasts I have ever had; big fluffy buttermilk biscuits with sausage gravy and eggs. In a big garden behind the house, my grandmother spent much time hoeing potatoes and gathering vegetables. She always wore calf length dresses and a thin housecoat. Before going out to the garden to work, she would get a big chew of Red Man tobacco, a habit among many of the older mountain folk. She carried her tobacco pouch in the front pocket of her house coat and sometimes would give me a small leaf to chew. I loved spending time in the garden with my granny, no matter whether I was helping to pick vegetables or pull weeds.

I especially remember my grandmother teaching me how to harvest potatoes and how hard I tried not to cut into the potatoes with the hoe. When I did, I would hastily cover the potato with dirt in hopes that my grandma wouldn't find it, not because I was scared of getting in trouble but because I didn't want to disappoint her. She would always recheck where I had been hoeing and find the cut potatoes even after I hid them. She never reprimanded me but simply placed them in a separate bucket and said, "Looks like we will be having mashed potatoes for supper tonight, Sweetie." After dinner, she usually spent time with me in the evening and told fascinating stories. After one or two, she would tuck me into bed and say a bedtime prayer before turning out the lights. Unlike the case with my grandmother, I can't remember a time when my birth mother was there to tuck me in, hug me, or even play with me.

My mother, Veronica Jo Butler, had long brown hair and hazel eyes. She was in and out of my life a lot as a child. She was born in 1958. Even though my grandparents had several other children, Veronica came along later in their lives and thus grew up more or less as an only child. I imagine that she was quite spoiled due to the untimely passing of her sister Ruthie Mae. Veronica disliked school and dropped out after the eighth grade, never returning to earn her GED. Early in her teenage years, she began partying with friends, staying out late, and worrying her parents to death. She met her husband-to-be, Willard Simms, a few years before I was born. Veronica was only fifteen when she first met Willard at a bible camp in 1973.

Willard was a year older than Veronica. He was a tall man, standing six feet and five inches, and he weighed about two hundred and twenty-five pounds. Like Veronica, Willard never made it through high school, finishing only the tenth grade. He always wore dark blue jeans, cowboy boots, and western style shirts. Willard Simms was known to many as an extremely temperamental person with an aggressive personality that was fueled even further by alcohol consumption. There were early warning signs that he was an abusive man. On one occasion Willard hit Veronica for talking to a guy outside her home in Lawford. Subsequently, after he found a letter that Veronica had written to another guy, Willard drove her down a long dirt road and put a pistol to her head, threatening to kill her for writing the letter. She escaped this harrowing situation by telling Willard that if he shot her, her dad would kill him. Veronica and Willard dated for a short time in 1973 and parted only a few months after first meeting each other.

After the breakup, Veronica met my biological father, Tim Boyd, a thirty-year-old married man. At age sixteen she entered into an adulterous relationship with this man. After several intimate encounters with John, she became pregnant with me, the first of her four children. After being informed of the pregnancy, John wanted nothing to do with Veronica or the unborn child. He was interested only in sexual encounters with a girl half his age and had no desire to start a second family or support an illegitimate child. Veronica never spoke to John again after notifying him of the pregnancy, and throughout my childhood I never knew who my biological father was. Even with an infant daughter, Veronica continued to date other men, but she never forgot Willard Simms, nor would he let her.

Willard, meanwhile, had become involved with another woman soon after he broke up with Veronica in 1973. Willard's new girlfriend, Susan Kidman, had been dating him for a short while before she announced that she was pregnant. Upon this news, Susan's mother insisted that the two get married. The pregnancy claim turned out to be false, but the two married in 1974 as planned. The marriage produced two children, both girls, born about a year apart. The first child was born just two days after me in the same hospital. In fact, Willard and Veronica crossed paths at the hospital during this time, casually conversing before going their separate ways. The marriage between Susan and

Willard was not idyllic. Susan experienced some abuse at the hands of her husband, but nothing like what he would prove capable of in the years to come.

In 1977, Willard and Veronica started to see each other again. An illicit relationship soon commenced, and Veronica became pregnant with her second child within a few months. Willard now had two children by Susan and one on the way with Veronica. The affair was more than Susan could endure, and Willard soon found himself divorced and settling into a long-term relationship with Veronica. After the birth of her son, Sammy Ross Simms, in July of 1978, Veronica was ready to settle down and give family life a chance, but Willard was still emotionally and physically involved with Susan. Both Veronica and Susan were aware of his promiscuous behavior, but they allowed it to go on for several months. During this period Susan had some discussions with Veronica about what she had endured at the hands of Willard and warned her not to marry him. In September of 1978, Susan met another man and ended the sexual relationship with Willard. Angry at being rejected, Willard moved back to his hometown of Pennsboro and asked Veronica to live with him.

The following month Veronica and her infant son Sammy moved to Pennsboro to be with Willard. After living there for only a short while, Willard and Veronica decided to get married. Against the advice of Willard's ex-wife, Veronica married him in the spring of 1979 when I was only four years old. Veronica, Willard, and their one-year-old son moved to the small community of Auburn a few weeks after they married. Auburn was less than ten miles from Lawford, but we only saw them when they came to our house to eat, do their laundry, or ask for money. From the very start, they had a rocky relationship. Only two months after their wedding Willard accused Veronica of having an affair and sought a separation. As a result, Veronica and Sammy moved in with me and my grandparents in the summer of 1979. My grandparents always helped Veronica as much as they could, since she had little education, no job, and a child to support. Though I too was her child, she never supported me. I would never truly be a part of Veronica's family, and that was fine by me. Thankfully, her stay in Lawford was short.

Willard moved from Auburn after the separation and got his own apartment in Pennsboro. Once again he started visiting Veronica in Lawford and soon asked her to reconcile. Against the advice of her parents, Veronica moved to Pennsboro to give the marriage another try. After several months of moving from place to place, Veronica and Willard found their way back to the Cox Mills area where they rented a small camper trailer. Cox

Mills was only about seven miles from Lawford, where I lived until my grandfather passed away in February of 1981.

I will never forget watching my grandfather take his last breath. I was only five years old, and my little heart was breaking. My grandfather was sitting in the living room in his favorite chair when he died. I remember crying out to him, "Wake up, Paw-Paw, wake up." Willard grabbed me by the arm, pushed me back, and said, "Shut up dummy. Can't you see he's dead?" I never liked Willard much but after my grandfather's death, I wished that Veronica's husband would just disappear. My life, as well as my grandmother's life, would forever change after Houston passed away.

CHAPTER 3

Imaginary World

A few months after my grandfathers' passing, my granny and I had to move in with Veronica and Willard in the small camper until we could find another place to live. I don't know why we had to move from the house in Lawford, but one thing that was for sure was the move would bring a big change in lifestyle. My grandmother and I stayed in the camper for only a few weeks, but I got a taste of what life with Veronica and Willard would be like. I was ready to move out the day we moved in. Living conditions in the little camper were crowded, and my granny and I were made to feel like a huge burden. Three adults and two children living in a small camper were more than Willard could deal with, and his simmering rage kept me and my grandmother in constant fear.

Willard never cared much for me as a child. In fact, he was downright hateful to me. He gave me mean looks every time he got a chance, for which reason I never spoke to him because I was afraid of how he might react. Fear would overtake me as he peered toward me through his black framed glasses. He would walk by me and slap me in the head when nobody was around and call me names like "little redheaded brat" and "redheaded trash." He would just stare at me after he hit me, his nostrils flared, and anger just seethed out of him. I was terrified of Willard, and he knew it. The fear that I felt when I was in his presence was like nothing I have ever felt before. This might be why Veronica never wanted me to stay with them. She probably knew that I would fall victim to his abusive ways and would be better off with my grandmother. Sometimes I thought that he didn't like me simply because I was not his child. In any case, the dislike was mutual. My grandmother disliked him as well, and she knew she had to get a place of her own before something bad happened.

After living in the camper with Veronica and Willard for several weeks, my grandmother and I moved into a small rental house in Cox Mills a few miles away. Life there was much different for both of us. Granny was now seventy years old, and I was almost six. The house had no indoor plumbing or running water, only an old outhouse in the back yard that I was scared to use. I did all my "business" sitting on a bucket on the back porch. Since the tiny house had no central heat, my grandmother had to turn on all four stove burners to warm the small house. During the winter months, I customarily slept in blue jeans and a flannel shirt. For water we had a well and sometimes we drank water straight from the draw bucket using a long handled dipper. I also remember taking baths in a big metal tub in the cramped kitchen. After we carried water into the house pail by pail, my granny would heat it on the stove and mix it with cold water before bathing me. We obviously were very poor in 1981, but I was too young to know it. We would eat beans and cornbread one night, and the next day granny would make fried bean cakes with the leftovers.

An old man named Roy lived a while down from us, and sometimes I visited him because there were no other children nearby. He always would offer me a chew of tobacco. One day I took him up on the offer and took a big hunk, much bigger than the small leaf of tobacco my granny would give me. I figured that if my sweet little granny chewed the stuff, why shouldn't I? Big mistake, it made me so sick that I couldn't see straight. With no one my age to play with, I was a very lonely child, though one day out of the blue came along an imaginary friend. His name was Dino, and he appeared out of nowhere. He would sit on my shoulder; we would go for walks and play together in the woods, and he would help me with my homework.

He sometimes showed up at school during recess time, even when there were kids around. I soon learned that, when you are poor, kids can be very cruel, so having a friend like Dino was helpful. He didn't care that I was poor and maybe a little dirty, or that I had red hair and freckles. He liked me just the way I was.

During the time we lived in Cox Mills, we saw very little of Veronica and Willard. I do remember a time when they came to our house, the two of them fighting as usual, and Willard held my granny and Veronica hostage. Hearing them arguing outside, I looked out the window to see what was happening. Granny was sitting in her truck while Willard was stalking around the truck with a big revolver in his hand. I was scared to death and hid under my granny's bed during the conflict, praying to God to please help us. When I heard the gun go off, I remember thinking that Willard had shot my grandmother. I later found out that he had fired in the air to intimidate them while he was holding them hostage. After a few hours, Willard left with Veronica and granny came back into the house unharmed. So many times I wished that Willard would go away and never come back.

While we both missed my grandpa very much, we were doing the best we could to start our new life in Cox Mills. My grandmother received money from my grandfather's Social Security benefit, in addition to a monthly black lung check from the Coal Miners Union. She drew about eight hundred dollars per month, which was enough to keep the lights on and food on the table for the two of us. A large portion of her modest income went to help Veronica and Willard, and believe me they were there every month to collect.

Other memories of that time and place include Page's General Store about a mile down the road. Mr. Page delivered groceries to us about once a week. He was a kind man who always brought me a Whatchamacallit candy bar and a bag of Mister Bee's sour cream and onion potato chips. We had no means of transportation since my grandmother never had learned how to drive, nor could we have afforded a car. Therefore, we walked half a mile each way to the church that she and my grandfather had attended for many years. My uncle was the preacher there, and although I didn't know him well, he seemed like a good man. I particularly remember that he had beehives behind his house and occasionally would bring us a jar or two of honey with the comb still in the jar. For some reason, I was always fascinated by the honeycomb.

Old man Jack, another figure from that time, used to walk up and down the road in front of our house, every day picking up cans from the roadside and hanging them upside down on nearby tree limbs. When I asked my grandmother what he was doing, she just smiled and shook her head. I guess she didn't really know either. He was a harmless old man who never said anything to me, though once in a while he would throw his hand up at us. I was a little afraid of him but mostly just curious.

A small creek ran in front of the property where I used to go fishing. To make a pole, I found a sturdy stick in the woods, which granny then rigged with some thread and a hook. For bait, I would dig a couple of worms from the soft, rich dirt and take off to the creek. I caught much small fish from that stream, what my grandmother called "horny head chubs." I was so proud when I caught one that I would run up to the house just to show her my prize. She was always excited for me and made me feel special. Life must have been tough for her back then, but she never showed it. While she and I were settling into our new life in Cox Mills; Willard, Veronica, and Sammy were trying to find their own way just down the road.

There were increasing episodes of violence and abuse between Willard and Veronica. One night when they were arguing, Willard threw Veronica out of the camper into the pouring rain. Veronica sought shelter at the landlord's house until Willard agreed to let her come back. On another occasion, their fighting again turned violent when Willard struck Veronica in the face with his fist. Veronica ran from the camper to the landlord's house once again, this time with a split lip and a black eye. Chasing her across the yard, Willard was stopped at the front door by the landlord brandishing a double-barreled shotgun. The landlord said to Willard, "You go back down to the camper, young man before I put this gun to good use." The next day he told them they needed to find another place to live, and within a week they moved to the Cedar Creek area near Glenville, West Virginia.

While living there Willard and Veronica conceived their second child and in the summer of 1982, Veronica gave birth to a girl named Sara. Although their family was growing, the abuse was increasing. The couple had started experimenting with group sex as well as mail-order sexual encounters. Both were involved with another couple and had group sexual relations several times during this period. They then placed an ad in an adult magazine requesting an exchange of pornographic letters and photos. Correspondence, pictures, and sometimes money came to them in the mail each week. They spent the money on beer and cigarettes and placed the pictures in a scrapbook that Veronica had started. The letters and photos soon led to an actual meeting. Willard and Veronica had invited a couple from Chicago to visit them at their home in Cedar Creek, a "casual encounter" that occurred in the summer of 1984. During this one week visit the two couples had sexual relations several times. They also took pictures for the adult scrapbook. As a young child, I had the extreme misfortune of happening upon this compendium. Many of the photos were of Veronica, Willard, and several others I had never seen before engaged in explicit sexual positions. Some, though, were of bestiality involving people and dogs. This was the most devastating thing I had ever seen. It forever burned images into my mind that no child, or adult for that matter, should ever see.

The sexual experimentation and past abuse triggered more problems for Veronica and Willard in the months to come. On one occasion they were in the process of transporting a washing machine in the back of a truck when the washer tipped over. Willard naturally became enraged and blamed Veronica, striking her in the face with his fist and giving her a black eye during the argument that ensued. Willard's brother, Albert, was so appalled that he left after condemning Willard's behavior. While Willard and Veronica continued their dysfunctional ways in Cedar Creek, my grandmother's health was deteriorating and she began to need more help with day-to-day activities. After living in Cox

Mills for three years, we soon had to move again when I was eight years old; launching a three-year period of instability that would change my life forever.

CHAPTER 4

The Move

In the fall of 1984, my granny and I moved in with Veronica and Willard at Cedar Creek. They had been living there for over a year when we went to stay with them. The first day there was horrible. Amid the constant arguing, Veronica tried her best to get my grandmother involved, but she would always take the kids into the bedroom or tell us to go outside. Many times the arguments turned violent when Willard slapped or hit Veronica. After he beat her, he would write a love note or buy her some flowers to make up for the abuse. It was a vicious cycle that would go on for years.

Behind the small house perched on a hillside was a gully that held old rusty stoves and refrigerators. Soon after we moved in I accidentally let my favorite ball roll down into the gully. It was a big, rubber, pink ball of the kind you find in a grocery store. My granny had bought it for me when we lived in Cox Mills. Knowing how much that ball meant to me, Willard forbade me to go down into the gully to retrieve it. Every day I would sit on the back porch and see my pink ball. My fear of a severe beating kept me from violating Willard's directive. Willard routinely called me a "little redheaded brat" and beat Sammy and me for the smallest thing. He was not working during this time; thus, was always at the house. Life was a living nightmare for all of us with him around. Because Willard had no job, we subsisted on welfare and food stamps. We also ate a lot of wild game back then, squirrel and deer meat were a common meal. Once I remember walking past the laundry room and seeing a skinned squirrel sitting upright. To this day I have no idea how it happened, but the sight scared me to death. I guess that Willard skinned the poor thing alive. Veronica would put a huge pot of water on to boil and place the entire squirrel into the pot. It was just awful. I shouldn't complain, I suppose. At least we had something to eat, even if only every couple of days or so.

While living in Cedar Creek I began fourth grade at Normantown Elementary, which I hated partly because I had to wear long sleeve flannel shirts to school even when it was hot outside. I can remember my teachers asking me why I was wearing the flannel shirts, and all I could think to say was, "I am cold." I was embarrassed because the truth was that I didn't have any shirtsleeve shirts. We shopped at the Salvation Army store, and it seemed as though everyone at school knew. The other children made fun of me because they realized that I was poor. The black trash bag I used to carry my books in was probably the giveaway. When I told Veronica about the ridicule, Willard called me a "spoiled little redheaded brat" and advised me saying, "Get tough or drop out of school like I did." He had no kind words to offer either me or my half-brother. It hurt my grandmother deeply to see us being abused, and things did not get any better until my grandmother and I moved to another part of the state.

We lived at Cedar Creek for about six months before migrating to Cyclone, West Virginia. I imagine that my grandmother could no longer stand Willard's beating me, so she asked her son if he would come to get us. I was still in fourth grade, but I was excited about escaping from Cedar Creek. I will never forget when my granny told me that her son, Melvin, was coming up to take us away. The first thing I did when I found out that we were leaving was to run down into the gully and get my pink ball. A few hours later Melvin pulled up in a red Chevy truck with a camper cover over the bed. Granny and I were ready to hit the road just a few minutes after he arrived. I was so happy to be in the back of that old truck bouncing my ball against the tailgate and watching the house of horror disappear as we drove off. We were on our way to Cyclone to start a new life.

Cyclone was over 100 miles to the south of Cedar Creek, not too far from Beckley, West Virginia. My grandmother had three adult sons living in this area, and they thought it would be better if we got away from Veronica and Willard. They knew how mean Willard could be and feared that their mother and I could be in danger. Cyclone was definitely a backwoods country. We rented a trailer that was deep in a holler. We had very few neighbors, and the ones we did have were several hundred yards away. Still, we were only a short walking distance from Melvin's house, where on some nights we would have dinner together. Everyone in the holler chewed tobacco or dipped snuff, so soon after we moved there I experimented with dipping snuff. I loved the Gold River snuff. Although I was only eight or nine years old at the time, my granny would buy me a three pack, and I would get a "dip" as soon as I could open the can. Life in Cyclone was much different than before, and the funny thing was that I seemed to fit in better with the kids at school. While plenty of things were going on in my life that should not have happened, I at least was free from the physical and emotional abuse I had experienced in Cedar Creek. I prayed that we would never have to be around Willard and Veronica again, but unfortunately my prayers went unanswered.

During the summer after I completed fourth grade we had to move back in with Veronica, Willard, Sammy, and Sara. Granny said that they needed help paying the bills and wanted her to look after the two grandchildren while they looked for work. Melvin begged her not to go, as did I, but she had a heart of gold and wished to do what she could to help Veronica. Meanwhile, they had left Cedar Creek and moved into a trailer in the village of Sago near Hampton, West Virginia. We were there for only a short period of time, but I took away more bad memories from my time in Sago. While we were living there, Willard gave me a severe beating for no reason. I had asked Veronica if I could go across the railroad tracks with my friend Annie to pick blackberries. I often walked the tracks and thought nothing of it, as did Veronica. When Willard got home; however, and saw me across the tracks, he came to get me. Because Annie was terrified of him, she took off running for home. The next thing I knew I was being lashed with a leather belt across the back of my legs, back, head, and arms, resulting in pronounced whelps and bruising. Apparently someone in the community had seen what he was doing to me and called the Department of Social Services. Unfortunately, they closed the case after a perfunctory investigation without taking any action against Veronica or Willard. My hatred towards Willard grew more intense with every minute I had to spend around him.

Another bad memory dating back to Sago involves a school fundraiser. While in the fifth grade I had brought home a brochure and asked Veronica whether I could sell candy for the school. She looked at the paperwork and agreed to help me. I was surprised and elated that Veronica wanted to spend time with me. The money I collected from our neighbors in the trailer park was supposed to pay for what they had ordered, but Veronica took all the money and spent it on cigarettes and beer. We moved again before the neighbors, or the school, realized what had happened. I can imagine the horrible things our former neighbors said about us after we moved.

We next arrived in Frenchton, a small community about five miles from Sago where we lived in a three bedroom rental house. Veronica and Willard were thinking about buying the house but could never come up with the money to close the deal. Times were tough, and there seemed to be no end to the madness. I remember one night Willard had gotten drunk and decided to drive his motorcycle through the front door of the house and after several failed attempts he became so enraged with Sammy and me for laughing that he began beating us with an extension cord. As a result, I had large whelps and severe bruising all over my back, and the backs of both my legs. To this day I can still remember the sting I felt as the cord struck against my body. Both my granny and I deeply feared Willard's propensity to violence and were planning to move back to Cyclone as soon as we could find transportation. In the summer of 1985, Veronica and Willard's marriage was quickly spiraling out of control.

While there, Veronica had become involved with a younger man, Dean Williams, and decided to leave Willard. Veronica, Dean, Granny, and all the children, myself included, loaded up in the Jeep and headed to Cyclone that October. Apparently Veronica had taken some money and a handgun with her. I thought that she had finally broken free from Willard and was embarking on a new life with Dean. Shortly after the move, however, Willard drove to Cyclone and demanded his two kids, his .38 caliber pistol, and any money she had taken before leaving Frenchton. After an intense confrontation between the two, Willard left Cyclone with Sammy, Sara, the pistol, and one hundred dollars. When Willard got back to Frenchton, he met with an attorney and filed divorce papers. He was seeking full custody of the two children and specified Veronica's infidelity as grounds for a divorce. In addition, Willard also asked for child support and for Veronica to pay his attorney fees. Veronica was not ready to let Willard have the children and viewed the divorce papers as a serious threat to her livelihood. After all, she was totally dependent on the welfare check that came with having the children in her custody. Not long after the divorce papers were served, she decided to reconcile with Willard and soon returned to Frenchton as a broken woman. Dean went to stay with his brother, never to speak again with Veronica after their affair.

I remember the day as if it were yesterday, Veronica and Dean packing up their clothes to begin the journey back to Frenchton. It was a rainy, dreary day. I had begged Veronica not to leave. I wanted my mom to be with me and I had also begun to grow somewhat fond of Dean. I had longed endlessly for a family, a mom and dad. I thought that if they would stay with my grandmother and me, then we would be just that—a family. Dean was always real nice to me, and Veronica seemed to be more tolerable and less on edge when she was away from Willard. I felt a sense of happiness if that was even possible, but on this day as they were pulling out of the driveway, I imagined I would never see either of them again. Willard was so angry at Veronica for what she had done, and I knew Dean would probably not be hanging around much longer especially knowing Veronica was going to give the marriage another try. I watched from my bedroom window as they pulled away, the rain falling even harder. I begin crying, I cried so hard, for such a long period of time, I became sick. My grandmother tried comforting me, but no comfort could be found. She loved me so much, I imagine she knew how I felt. I loved my granny dearly, and while I was happy to be there with her, I deeply desired to have the family unit that I had longed for my entire young life.

Because of the abuse I suffered at the hands of my stepfather, I never wanted to go back to live with Willard and Veronica. Veronica was not content to leave me and my granny alone. The phone calls asking for money were relentless. She always wanted money and worked hard to make sure she got it. My grandmother knew that the marriage was not going well because Veronica sent letters detailing Willard's horrific actions. I then overheard her talking to Veronica on the telephone about the financial troubles they were having in Frenchton. Veronica revealed that they had fallen behind on the rent and were looking for yet another place to live. Being more than three hundred dollars behind on rent, Veronica and Willard moved with their children to Adrian, just a few miles south of Buckhannon in Upshur County. In January of 1986, Willard lost his job at the oil rigs and his family again had to rely on welfare and food stamps. At the time they were living at a slum called Holly Apartments, decidedly not the kind of place where one would want to raise a family or reconcile a broken marriage.

Veronica and Willard continued to struggle financially and pressured my grandmother to send them money. After numerous phone calls, she agreed to help out with their bills, but the calls did not end there. Veronica was experiencing continuous abuse by Willard. She had sent letters to granny requesting rat poison and had made several comments about wanting Willard dead when she was living with us in Cyclone. In fact, she had asked my grandmother to shoot him on more than one occasion. Veronica had persisted in making bad choices, and her financial situation went from bad to worse. This time, however, Veronica did what I had dreaded. She insisted that we move back in with them again in Adrian. I asked myself over and over why we had to go back. I knew my fate at the hands of Willard. He would do as he had always done, beat me and call me names. I had thought of running away on several occasions, entertaining the idea of hiding in the mountains, but the thought of leaving my grandmother was more than I could bear. I loved her dearly, and where she went I would follow.

In February of 1986, Veronica came to Cyclone to take my granny and me back to Adrian. Veronica and Willard wanted my grandmother's money so badly that they figured the only way to get it was to have her move back in with them. My grandmother was now seventy-five years old, and I was only ten. I always felt like an outcast in my own mother's house. She had brought Sammy with her to pick us up, and we fought the entire time we were in the Jeep traveling back to Adrian. Although she was almost four months pregnant with her fourth child, Veronica still managed to pull over to the side of the road to beat me and Sammy with a stick for misbehaving in the back seat. Sammy was starting to act and talk just like Willard. I was terrified of the future and sad about leaving Cyclone, the only place I felt safe. I knew that the days of not being used as a punching bag were soon to end and that I was about to experience tough times at the hands of my neglectful mother and abusive stepfather.

When we pulled into the driveway, Willard was standing on the front stoop with a cigarette hanging out of his mouth and his arms crossed, looking at us as though we were nothing but trash. Sara was in the house crying, and he yelled to Veronica, "Get your sorry self in this house and take care of this squalling baby." I knew right then that things had not changed between Veronica and Willard. Willard didn't want us around at all, but he was happy to take my grandmother's money. On our first night in Adrian, he asked my grandmother how much money she had and took fifty dollars from her purse to buy gas, beer, and cigarettes. He even had the nerve to ask me if I had any money. I remember carrying around two quarters in my pocket, but I was not going to give them to Willard Simms. He was the same hateful person he had always been, and there was no changing that. Even so, there was one bright spot in that phase of my life.

Not long after we had moved back to Adrian, I was outside playing in front of the apartments when I saw a white Chevrolet S-Ten pull up. Out stepped a tall, distinguished looking gentleman in his mid-thirties with salt-and-pepper hair and a smile so genuine that I was immediately drawn to him. I ran up to him and wrapped my arms around his leg. He said his name was Brother Jim and asked whether my parents were home. He was the pastor of a church in Rock Cave called New Covenant Baptist Church, and he wanted to know if my family and I would like to attend Vacation Bible School. I told him I would love to. I went inside and got Veronica, who told him that if I wanted to go she didn't mind. So every day for a week that summer he showed up, and we had Vacation Bible School at Holly Apartments. After it was over, I wanted to go to church with Brother Jim. I asked Veronica about the idea, she said that I would not have a way to get there; but, Brother Jim offered to pick me up. I was so excited that I could barely contain myself. I ran and told Sammy about it and he said that he wanted to go too. I didn't know much about God; I just knew that if I prayed for what I needed, he would help me. This visit by Pastor Jim McCall was truly an answer to prayer. God was always looking out for me; I just didn't know it at the time.

When Sunday rolled around, Brother Jim picked us up just as he said he would. He took several of the children in the surrounding community to church and then dropped us off afterward. This was the beginning of some of the most wonderful memories of my young life. Jim and his wife Mrs. Kay treated us so kindly. Never had I felt this kind of love and genuine compassion before. As time went on, I grew more and more attached to them, so much so that I wanted them to be my family. I began to believe that God had given me the father I never had. When Pastor McCall hugged me, it made me feel as though everything in my crazy little world was going to be okay. I begin to develop a very special relationship with Jim, talking to him about some of the things I was dealing with at home. When I begged him not to take me home, he would simply say, "Mary, you know that I have to take you back." I knew he had to, but why? I hated going back to that house of horror.

Not long after I started going to church, I thought about getting baptized. I talked to Brother Jim, and he asked me several questions about accepting Jesus into my heart. After I told him I had done so, he said that he would be glad to baptize me. A few weeks later I was baptized. It was wonderful to feel as though I were part of something. I worked hard every week to memorize Bible verses. I wanted to make Mrs. Kay proud of me, and she always told me what a great job I did. Even though Sammy and I attended church regularly, neither Veronica nor Willard ever went with us. There was little room for spirituality in their lives. Willard spent most of his time drinking beer and hanging out in town with his buddies, while Veronica was busy doing much the same thing. Whenever she got a chance she went to her friends' apartment, a "sin den" where she fit in well. In time, all of us had outgrown the two-bedroom apartment and within a few months would relocate yet again.

CHAPTER 5

The Rat Trap

In July of 1986, we moved into a rental house just across the road from Holly Apartments. As you walked in the front door, there was a small living room and off to the right an equally small bedroom. In the middle was the dining room and across from it the other bedroom, which Sammy and Sara shared. The kitchen was in the rear. The back door by the kitchen opened into a thick wooded area. Whenever Willard was away, Veronica would put on her slippers and visit her friends across the road. Willard had forbidden her from going to the apartments without him, but now that she had her mother as a babysitter she felt free to roam. One night Willard came home while Veronica was visiting a friend at the apartments. He was seething with anger; he left and found her at Debbie Fisher's home. I remember watching out the window as he pulled Veronica back across the road by her hair. Although it was only seven o'clock in the evening, my grandmother and I got into our bed, which occupied the dining room and pretended to be sleeping before they came back. We stayed in bed the entire evening for fear of getting caught up in the fighting. We could hear them arguing for several hours. The next day Veronica had bruises on her arms, neck, and face. That afternoon Willard brought her wildflowers and told her he was sorry. Our lives had taken a change for the worse. It would only grow more intense as time passed.

Sammy and I was forever the target of beatings. Malnourished, we would often go hungry for days on end. In the sixth grade, I weighed a mere sixty pounds (the average weight for an elevenyearold girl is seventynine pounds). Veronica and Willard usually ate fast food, with little thought for the rest of us. Occasionally they would give our youngest sister a mayonnaise sandwich while Sammy and I would lie on the ground acting as though we were dying of starvation in hopes that Sara would give us just a small bite. We were not allowed to go into the kitchen for food. One day Sammy and I were walking down Gould Road and found a dollar bill lying on the side of the road. We were excited because we planned on buying ourselves a hot dog at the country store. We knew we had to ask permission to walk that far, so we approached Veronica. When she asked why we wished to make the trek, we told her that we had found a dollar and wanted to buy some food.

"Let me see," Veronica said. So, I took it out of my pocket. Hardly had I gotten the bill out before she snatched it from my hand and said, "You two go on back outside and play. I need this to buy me some cigarettes." Veronica's selfishness killed our hopes. After she took our dollar, I went outside, sat down, and cried. Sammy stayed in the house to see whether he could find food somewhere.

Sammy got into a kitchen cabinet, found a can of potted meat, and ate it all on his own. When Willard found the empty can in the trash, he went crazy. He did stuff like that because he wanted to control everything we did, and not allowing us to eat was part of his sick domination over us. He took both of us into the kitchen and made us stand there to confess who ate the food. We were both frightened, and he was fuming mad. Though we denied eating anything, he made us open our mouths so he could look. He then took out a rat trap, set the powerful spring bar, and threatened to chop off our fingers with the trap unless we admitted to eating the can of potted meat. I was trembling after he took a spoon and triggered the trap right in front of my face. He then reset the trap and said to me, "Put those thieving fingers on the wood so I can chop them off, you little redheaded brat." I was scared to death by this point. "No, please Willard," I pleaded. "I didn't eat the stuff, I swear to God. Sammy had to have eaten it because I was outside." Willard then turned his attention to Sammy and slammed the trap in his face to scare him into talking. Sammy was not going to admit to the deed, so we went back and forth blaming one another. When my grandmother walked into the kitchen and asked why he was doing this to us, he told her, "It's none of your business. Now get out of here, you old hag." Only a short time later he put the rat trap back under the cabinet and beat us both with a leather belt, all this over a can of potted meat. To this day I hate seeing a can of potted meat. Although there would be more violence in our future, for some reason nothing scared me as much as this incident.

Granny often tried to protect Sammy and me by saying to Willard, "Please. They're just little kids." Her efforts at intervention, however, led to Willard's hating my grandmother even more than he already did. On one occasion Sammy took the spring off the screen door and, while playing with, accidentally launched it into an overgrown wooded area. When Willard got home, he grabbed us both by the neck, hauled us outside, and told us to find the spring and not to come back into the house until we did. The following day he made us get up early in the morning and search for the spring until it was so dark that we could no longer see. Then, beat us every evening for not finding it. Of course, we went to bed hungry as usual and with no bath. This punishment went on for four straight days until my granny begged Willard to stop and promised to buy a new spring for the door. He said, "That's not the point. The little bastards need to find the one they lost." We never found it, but my granny did buy a new spring, which cost a whopping twenty-five cents at the local hardware store. Thankfully the beatings over the lost spring ended, but the abuse still continued.

One day Sammy was caught pulling down his pants in front of a little girl at Holly Apartments, and one of our neighbors told Willard what Sammy had done. Willard punished him by pouring black pepper in both his eyes and mouth. I remember the poor little guy screaming his head off, begging his father to please stop, but as usual it was all to no avail. After that Willard kicked Sammy all the way to his room and made him remain there for the rest of the evening. He never allowed Sammy to wash his mouth out or purge his eyes. My half-brother cried and cried. I wanted so badly to help him, but I was given strict orders to stay away from him.

In September of 1986, Veronica gave birth to a fourth child named Jacob Lee. He was a big boy, weighing over ten pounds, and I can remember how excited I was when he came home. I enjoyed caring for him very much, but to Veronica he was apparently just one more encumbrance. When she regularly went out partying, I was left to babysit Jacob. I didn't mind, but sometimes he would wake up at two or three in the morning and Veronica, if she had returned home, would be passed out in her bed. Under those circumstances, I would get up and try to comfort him as best I could. He may have been a little colicky, but how could a ten-year-old deal with that?

Our "family," such as it was, never celebrated birthdays. Not once did I get to blow out candles or even be wished a Happy Birthday. That was hardly surprising. There never were any happy times, so how could there possibly be a happy birthday? So here we were: four kids, my grandmother, and two adults who fought all the time living in a two bedroom house with one bathroom. This was more than Willard could handle. It seemed that he was constantly enraged, lashing out at all of us for no reason. I always tried not to get within arm's reach of him. Sometimes, if he walked by me, he would draw back his fist as though he were going to hit me. I would jump, or throw my arms up to protect myself, and he would laugh in my face. He really liked knowing that he had control.

I will never forget Christmas of 1986. Willard, Veronica, and all their kids went to Willard's ex-wife's house to celebrate the holiday. They spent the entire weekend with Susan, her new husband, and the two girls he and Susan had together. My grandmother had bought a turkey, but Willard and Veronica took it with them after leaving us at the small house in Adrian. Granny and I celebrated Christmas alone that year, which was fine by me. Christmas then was no different than any other day, but my present was the absence of Veronica and Willard. Besides, the last time I went to Susan's home Veronica had beaten me with a belt so hard that the buckle broke off when it struck my cheekbone. I think she did this to show Willard's ex just how tough she thought she was.

Shortly thereafter Willard found a new way to earn money. He had spotted an ad for a truck driving school in Virginia that offered guaranteed placement after a one month driving course. He decided to pay the two hundred and fifty dollars enrollment fee, which of course came from my grandmother. The driving course took him to Virginia, and we were glad to see him go. When he returned after the training class, he told Veronica that the job he had been offered was an over the road assignment. He would be gone two weeks at a time, but home every other weekend. Veronica was fine with that arrangement as long as he sent money to her so that she could pay the bills and buy beer and cigarettes. He agreed to send every other check back home.

While Willard was on the road, life became one big party. Veronica spent almost every evening at Holly Apartments while Sammy, Sara, Jacob Lee, and I spent most of our time staying with my granny in the small wood frame house. Sometimes I made my way over to the apartments and hung out with the adults. Sammy and I had plenty of opportunities to drink alcohol. After one time we both got sick and never experimented with it again. While there, Veronica was always sitting on other men's laps, whispering in their ears, and acting as if she were a teenager again. All the women and men were flirting with each other during these late-night parties at Holly Apartments. On one occasion Veronica and a girlfriend streaked around the apartments naked. From what I later learned, two young men were running around naked at the same time. Although I was not there, I remember Veronica's talking about the event with her friends a few days later. She must have had a lot of nerve, knowing that if Willard found out there would be a price to pay. I also remember Willard's striking Veronica with a belt at about this time for refusing to get one of the girls at Holly Apartments to have sex with him. This type of behavior was very common between them. There was no commitment or love in this marriage.

Veronica became quite fond of another guy during this period. Everyone called him Bo, but his real name was John Bowman. He had moved to Adrian from Georgia about two months after my grandmother and I moved in. He was staying with one of his friends at Holly Apartments when he first came to Upshur County. I remember seeing Veronica walking across the apartments' parking lot one night holding his hand. I found myself thinking that maybe Veronica would leave Willard for Bo. One night she had him over for dinner serving kielbasa, canned green beans, and instant mashed potatoes. When they were done, we were allowed to have what was left over. Needless to say, we ate everything. It was the best meal I can remember her cooking. In retrospect, it seems as though she was willing to do more for a male friend that she would for her own children. After dinner, Bo sat down in the living room and watched TV with all of us. If Willard had come home and witnessed this scene, he would have killed both of them and maybe the rest of us as well. I was so scared he would come home that I looked out the window every five minutes to make sure he was not pulling up in the driveway. After a while, the two of them went over to Holly Apartments to drink and party with all the others.

After about a week of seeing Bo, Veronica let him borrow the Jeep to move some things from the apartments to a house he was planning to rent a few miles toward Buckhannon. While he had the Jeep, Bo hit a patch of ice on the road and smashed into a big tree. A front fender was torn completely off, and the driver side mirror was dangling when he returned the vehicle a few hours later. He dropped off the Jeep in the driveway and vanished without telling us about the wreck. Veronica was furious about what had happened, but her anger quickly turned to fear when she thought about what Willard would do when he got home and saw the damage. The wreck occurred on a Thursday, and Willard was scheduled to be home on Saturday. Veronica had no time to get the fender or mirror repaired before he returned, and she knew what would occur. After she saw the damaged Jeep, she told me, "If we don't kill that bastard, he will kill all of us when he comes home." The fallout would trigger a weekend of violence and abuse like none other previously.

CHAPTER 6

The Last Weekend

Willard had called home Thursday evening after the wreck to check up on everything. He was somewhere in Pennsylvania when he called. Veronica told him that she had wrecked the Jeep after hitting a patch of ice on Old Miller Road. Willard was livid. From across the room, I could hear him screaming into the phone, calling Veronica stupid and telling her that he was going to "beat her senseless" when he got home on Saturday. I was terrified just hearing his voice. We spent the next day scripting the story we would tell him. On Friday night I prayed that something would happen to Willard's truck so that he would not make it home for the weekend. While I was saying my prayer, Veronica was back at the apartments drinking beer and hanging out with her friends until early in the morning.

Shortly after sunrise, Willard pulled into the driveway with a friend of his. I peeped out the front window and watched him, six feet and four inches tall; get out of the passenger side of the car. I was hopin that his friend would get out too, but after Willard slammed the door his friend pulled out of the driveway. Willard walked straight over to the wrecked Jeep to assess the damage. After staring at the fender for a few seconds, he started kicking the Jeep and muttering to himself. I was scared to death and ran back to bed where granny was still asleep. I snuggled as close to her as I could. As soon as Willard walked through the door, he started yelling for Veronica. He bellowed twice and then barged into the bedroom where she was sleeping. I could hear him telling her to wake up and asking her if she was still drunk. Suddenly I heard Veronica exclaim, "Don't do that to me, Willard please stop" and the next thing I heard was the sound of Willard's hand smacking her. Then I heard her say, "Willard, put the gun away before somebody gets killed." At this point, my baby brother Jacob woke up. As soon as I heard him moving around in his crib, I grabbed him and put him in the bed with granny and me. There followed quite a tussle in the bedroom, and I could hear things breaking as the two fought. Then everything went silent in the house. All I could think about was my mother lying dead. Thirty minutes later Veronica emerged from the bedroom with tears in her eyes and a busted lip.

She immediately went into the kitchen and swallowed some pain pills. I got out of the bed with

Jacob Lee and asked her if she needed me to do anything. Veronica told me to warm some milk for the baby and try to get him to sleep again. It was typical for her to want the baby to be asleep because then she wouldn't have to deal with him. I remember her saying, "he is going to die this weekend." Veronica proceeded to tell me, Sammy, and Sara to get dressed because she wanted us to stay outside all day so that Willard could sleep. It was February, the temperature hovering in the thirties, but we bundled up with what we had and made our way out the back door to play in the woods. By early afternoon on Saturday, Willard had awakened and was on the warpath again. He first went over to Holly Apartments and started knocking on everybody's door, asking questions about what had gone on while he was out of town. The more people he talked to, the angrier he became. Someone told him that his wife had been sleeping around during his absence. Another man told him that Bo had wrecked the Jeep and that Veronica had been seeing a lot of Bo. Willard was so mad when he came back that he went through the house throwing anything he could find. He grabbed Veronica, threw her against the wall, and started slapping her with the back of his hand. "You're lying," Willard said. "You're messing around on me again, and I'm going to kill you for it."

My grandmother was sitting at the kitchen table and shouted for him to stop slapping Veronica. Then he turned his anger toward her. When he threatened granny, she retorted, "If you touch me, I'll call the police and have you locked up." Willard then looked at her with a blank stare, drew back his hand, and hit her in the side of her head, causing irreversible hearing loss to her left ear. I was fuming with anger, but I knew there was no defending ourselves against this man. I would never forgive him for what he did to my granny. All I could see when I looked at him was a ruthless, coldhearted bastard. Not a day went by that he didn't beat one of us. It was as though he had some sadistic fetish. I couldn't help but think how good it would feel to punch him in the face, and as time went on I contemplated the idea of what Veronica had said the idea of Willard Simms being dead. Thankfully he went across the road to Holly Apartments and got someone to take him to the site where Veronica had told him the Jeep had been wrecked. When he returned, he told Veronica that there was no sign of an accident on Old Miller Road, and he insisted that she show him exactly where she had wrecked the Jeep. Veronica had not anticipated this possibility when she devised her cover story. Not being able to take him to where the accident occurred forced her to reveal that Bo was the one driving when the accident occurred. One can imagine how angry this made Willard. He was so enraged with Veronica that he went immediately into the kitchen and got hold of a butcher knife. Grabbing Veronica by the hair, he threw her onto the bed in the dining room where granny and I slept. She begged him not to kill her, saying, "Please, Willard. Don't do this. The kids are watching." His only response was "you're going to die they're next." There was never a question in my mind that he would, in fact, kill all of us. I vividly remember watching as Willard pushed the knife down toward Veronica's throat, while she held him by the forearms and pushed upwards with all the strength she had in her. With one swift motion of his right arm, her throat would have been sliced wide open. This went on for what seemed like hours, but it lasted only a few minutes before Willard finally let her up. Before Veronica could get herself together, he grabbed her by the shirt, pulled it over her head, and attempted to strangle her with it. Would this madness never end? I thought. He then punched her in the face and beat her on the arms before throwing her to the floor. As he headed across the road to Holly Apartments, Willard told Veronica that he was going over there to find a woman he could have sex with.

I often tried to imagine what Veronica was thinking when she brought my grandmother and me back to this place. She knew that Willard hated us and that his past was filled with abuse. Perhaps she simply didn't care, having become numb to his violence, but I lived in constant fear of my life. I never allowed myself to think ahead to the future because I was never sure I would have one. I wanted to believe that things would get better, even though there seemed little chance of that. When you wake up every day to further poverty, abuse, and violence you begin to question whether life is worth living.

Later that same evening we, as usual, hadn't eaten anything, and Veronica decided to go over to the apartments. Maybe she thought that Willard had calmed down, or maybe she figured that he wouldn't beat her anymore. In any event, we were all tired at this point. Sara had started to fall asleep on the couch, so I carried her into her bedroom and got her into bed. Sammy soon followed. Visibly upset, Granny was still sitting at the kitchen table. I remember asking her what we were going to do. She just said, "I don't know, honey." I then heard Jacob Lee starting to wake up. I told my grandmother that he probably needed his diaper changed, so I got him up, changed him, and fed him. After we played for a short while, he was soon back to sleep. While everything was still somewhat quiet, granny and I also went to bed. I lay in bed for the longest time, but I was so hungry that I couldn't drop off to sleep. I knew there was nothing in the house that I could eat. Besides, if I had gotten anything out of the kitchen, who knows what the repercussions might have been at this time. So I began to think, and I realized that in the refrigerator was a large can of Enfamil that had been opened. I, therefore, got up and grabbed one of my baby brother's bottles to fill it with a small amount of the milk. I then replaced what I had taken out of the can with water so that Veronica and Willard wouldn't notice the deficit. I also put a little water in the baby bottle and rushed back to bed as quickly as I could. If they came home, I could hide the bottle behind the bed or under my pillow.

Weighing a mere sixty pounds at eleven years of age, I was in desperate need of some form of nutrition, so I quietly tucked myself down close to my grandmother and began sucking the contents of the bottle. I was embarrassed, not wanting even my granny to know, but I remember thinking how good it was. I felt an overwhelming sense of guilt that I was taking milk from my baby brother. I knew, though, that Veronica received food stamps and would be able to buy Jacob more formula. It wasn't long before the bottle was empty, and I was all but sucking air. I hurriedly got up, rinsed out the bottle, and went back to bed. I felt full for a change, something I had not experienced in a long time. I finally could go to sleep. After a short while, Willard burst back into the house, and then he and Veronica were back at it again. He was yelling at her for following him over to the apartments, and she was crying. This continued for about twenty minutes or so. I believe they had both been drinking. Eventually, an eerie silence fell over the little house in Adrian.

I was looking forward to the next day, February 22, 1987, because I knew that Brother Jim would be at the house early to pick me up for Sunday school. After changing Jacob Lee's diaper and making sure he was fed, I woke Sammy up to ask him if he was going to church. He said he was. A short time later Brother Jim showed up and off we went. Sammy and I had never been so happy and eager to get out of the house. Sarah went to church with us sometimes, but if she weren't awake we never woke her. I started thinking about Jacob Lee and hoped he would be okay until I returned, even though deep in my heart I never wanted to return. Sammy and I had a good day at church, and I wasn't at all looking forward to church ending. I knew that Brother Jim had hands to shake and people to talk with after his sermon, so I figured that the longer it took him the better. Besides, Sammy and I were the last ones to be dropped off. About an hour later, Brother

Jim rounded us up from the churchyard and told us it was time to go. On the way home I didn't talk about anything that was happening at the house. Before I got out of his truck, I asked whether he would be coming back to pick us up for the evening service, and he said, "Of course, darling." Great, I thought. I have something to look forward to.

As I made my way into the house, it was obvious that the fighting had not relented. Stuff was strewn everywhere. I immediately went to check on Jacob Lee, and thankfully he was okay. He was lying in his crib cooing and playing with his toes. My grandmother was apparently watching him because Willard and Veronica were nowhere to be found, and Sara was outside picking dandelions. I wasn't sure what to do; the violence was far from over. Granny and I talked for a bit. She said that Willard had been punching Veronica all day, and she wasn't sure where they were. A few minutes later they both came into the house. He was yelling at her, "How could you let that punk drive my Jeep?" While walking past me, Willard slapped me across the face and said, "What are you looking at, you little redheaded brat?" He had often told Veronica that she must have found me in a dumpster somewhere. I honestly thought that if she did I wish she had just left me there. Living with both of them was far worse than living in a dumpster.

The fighting continued well into the evening, but before long Brother Jim was back to pick us up for church. I couldn't find Sammy anywhere, assuming that he was probably playing at Holly Apartments or fishing at the creek, so I went off to church with Brother Jim. This was my only reprieve from the madness, allowing me temporarily to be with people who actually cared about me. The church service lasted only about an hour and a half, maybe two hours, on Sunday evenings, and the time went by faster than I had hoped. On the way back to the house, I as usual was the last to be dropped off. I took advantage of the opportunity to ask Brother Jim not to take me back there. This time he asked whether something was going on, probably seeing the scared look on my face. I told him how Willard was upset at Veronica for letting a guy named Bo borrow the Jeep and wrecking it. I then told him I was frightened and didn't want to go back there. I had a hard time finding accurate words to describe the abuse, and to a born and bred Southerner like Brother Jim a beating was just a good old-fashioned spanking that you got when you were out of line. Moreover, the bruises I had were always in places that were concealed by my shirt or jeans. I knew that Pastor McCall had to take me home. He hugged me tightly, though. I told him I loved him, and he said he loved me too. I got out of his truck for what would be the last time and made the dreaded walk up to my front door.

The house looked much as it had before I left for church that evening. Veronica was sitting on the couch, her lip bleeding and her arms black and blue. Willard was not there, thank God. When Sammy came out of his bedroom and asked me why I had gone to church without him, I told him that I couldn't find him. He was upset, of course, as I would have been too. In the kitchen granny was sitting at the table smoking a cigarette and drinking a cup of coffee. Veronica called to me from the living room and told me to check on Jacob, who needed his diaper changed. After that, we played for a while. As I looked at him, I wondered whether all the fighting and arguing could somehow be affecting him. What would become of him? Would he be a victim just like the rest of us? Would he go hungry as we did? Though I was reluctant to think of my own future, I couldn't help but reflect on his. Because it was starting to get late, I gave Jacob Lee a warm bath and dressed him snuggly in a yellow Winnie the Pooh jumper. With his bottle, he soon was fast asleep. The next day was a school day, so I was eager to get to bed myself. I woke up on Monday, February 23, prepared to catch the bus to school, but Veronica told me I would be staying home to help with Jacob Lee. Needless to say, I was a bit upset, for school was my only opportunity to get some food. Granny would sometimes give me thirty-five cents so that I could buy a snack out of the vending machine. She knew that Veronica and Willard starved us, but there was little she could do. When Veronica would see her mother giving me a little change, she would forbid her to do it, saying it wasn't fair to the rest of the kids. I always shared everything I had with Sammy anyway, and Sara never went without much. As the favorite, she got a sandwich or whatever she wanted pretty much when she wanted it. Sammy and I had to fend for ourselves.

Sammy wanted to stay home too, so Veronica let him, which made Willard mad. He complained bitterly about it, but eventually the tempest blew over. The one thing that didn't blow over was the wrecked Jeep, and it wasn't long before Willard was yelling and cursing again. This time, however, I saw a look in his eyes unlike anything I had seen before. He just couldn't or wouldn't let this matter go. It was not even nine in the morning when Willard started drinking. He was back and forth all day long between the house and the apartments as the fighting continued. Sammy, Sara, and I remained outside playing for much of the day. We were about the only kids there since everyone else was in school.

At about half past three in the afternoon, the bus dropped off the neighborhood kids, who soon were outside as well. Sammy and I were thirsty, so we went inside to get a drink of water. After hearing Willard and Veronica arguing again, Sammy and I sat down on the couch in the living room, just before Willard stormed out to the front porch cursing and yelling. Scared by the eruption, we wondered why we had ventured back into the epicenter. Bursting back into the house, Willard started asking Sammy and me if we knew who Bo was. We were afraid that if we said yes his rage would increase even more and that if we lied he would beat us mercilessly. He demanded that we tell him what we knew, so we told Willard we had seen Bo a couple of times. He then wanted to know if we had seen Veronica kissing him. We told him no, even though only days earlier Veronica and Bo had been sitting on the couch holding hands and kissing. I knew that they had done more than just kiss. That Veronica enjoyed the company of men was blatantly obvious even to an eleven year old. Maybe the fact that she was twenty-six and had four children was more than she could bear, but being a mother was on the very bottom of her priority list. Willard continued to drill us for answers, and it soon became obvious that we were not giving him the ones he wanted. Shortly thereafter he called his brother and then his ex-wife Susan asking if they could watch the kids for a few days. Neither of them could, for one rea son or another, enraging Willard even more. He got up and left once again. After perhaps an hour he returned with a bottle of vodka and a jug of orange juice. I remember Sammy's asking if we could have some, but Willard said, "No– now get out of my face." He was pretty intoxicated at this point, stumbling and verbally abusing all of us.

Sickeningly, Willard then walked over to Jacob Lee lying in his crib. When Veronica said, "Please don't wake him, Willard. He's sleeping." Her husband responded, by slapping Veronica. I know what I can do to get to you," picking up Jacob Lee and threatening, "I'll just kill him. After all, he's probably not mine anyway." Veronica tried to calm Willard down as best she could, finally succeeded in getting Jacob back into his crib. At this point, I was shaking and unable to believe that Willard's anger had finally targeted this helpless baby. After refilling his glass with vodka and a dash of orange juice, Willard again cursed Veronica and insisted that she be gone by the time he got back, and then he abruptly left. Veronica's mind instantly went back to the time she left Willard and went to Cyclone with Dean Williams where she received divorce papers threatening her livelihood.

This time he would be gone for several hours, but we knew what things would be like the minute he walked back through the door. After telling Sammy and Sara to get ready for bed, Veronica asked me to stay up for a little while and talk to her. She wanted to hold Jacob Lee for a while before he went back to sleep. Her arms hurt so badly from the beatings that I had to pick him up from the crib and lay him in her arms. She had something to talk to me about. She asked me to do what I knew had needed to be done for a long time—kill Willard Simms. If we didn't do something soon, it was obvious that he would kill one or more of us. Surely, if he could threaten his own infant son just to get back at Veronica, he would have no qualms about emptying his .45 caliber pistol into the rest of us. I knew intuitively, beyond a shadow of a doubt, that it was a case of either kill or be killed. I thus felt no anxiety when talking with Veronica about killing Willard. No remorse entered my mind. I was officially numb to the bastard. I hated the very ground his feet walked on. In my eyes, he was unworthy of even another day of life.

CHAPTER 7

Final Moments

When Willard finally returned at around half past eleven on Monday night, he immediately demolished the coffee table with his fist. The plastic cups Sammy and I had set there earlier that day went flying across the room. He said to Veronica, "I thought I told you to be gone when I got back!" Veronica sat on the couch in numb silence. You could see the life in her had been completely drained out; she had a look this time like none other I had ever seen. He then stumbled into the kitchen and made himself another drink. I just so happened to walk in there before he did, and he reared his hand back and slapped me across the face. When I started crying, Willard yelled at me to "shut up." He then told Veronica that she hadn't cooked a thing all day and needed to fix him some food. She protested that her arms were too sore from the beatings she had sustained, and she asked me to prepare some sauerkraut and weenies. When Veronica took the food to him, he threw it on the floor and told her, to now clean it up."

Willard sat in his favorite chair in the living room while continuing his tirade. By this time it was getting into the early morning hours of Tuesday, February 24th. Willard slipped in and out of consciousness as a result of the alcohol; however, the last thing he said to her before passing out was "I am going to kill you." I was sitting on the love seat across from my mother. We enjoyed several moments of silence, something we had not known in a very long time. When I started to nod off, Veronica said, "Mary, wake up. I need to talk to you." She then asked me to get the rifle out of her bedroom closet. After I brought it to her, she sat the gun next to her like a trophy before draping it with an old coat lying on the sofa. We sat quietly in the dark awaiting Willard's demise, but I knew that if the deed were to happen I would have to do it. Veronica had been beaten so badly that she couldn't even hold a cup of coffee, let alone a gun.

I knew that Veronica was waiting for just the right moment. When she carried the gun into the kitchen I asked, "Do you want me to do it?" (She had been asking me this off and on for some time). She said, "Yes, I do." She added that she wanted me to shoot Willard in the head, but I immediately objected. "What if it splatters on the wall? I don't want to see that," I protested. I then told her that I would shoot him in the chest. "Just make sure he's dead," Veronica responded. I felt sure that, if he didn't die that night, one of us would be killed whenever Willard woke up from his drunken stupor.

Rifle in hand, I walked down the hall from the kitchen, eager to put an end to this madness. All the memories of Willard's abusive ways and his treatment of my grandmother were spinning through my mind as I traversed the dining room where granny was fast asleep. I assumed a position next to Willard and put the gun up to his chest, the muzzle only a few inches away from his body. My heart pounding furiously, I pulled the trigger, but nothing happened. I ran back to the kitchen and told my mother that it wouldn't fire, whereupon she grabbed the gun, made an adjustment, and sent me back to try again. This time I walked with even more purpose back down the hall. All I kept thinking about was what would happen if he came and saw me standing there with a rifle pointed at him. Once I reached the living room I quickly positioned myself and pulled the trigger, but astonishingly nothing happened. I hurried back to the kitchen again, telling my mother that I didn't want to do this, but if I had to she needed to make sure it went off this time. My heartbeat racing, nauseated, my chest tight, I again walked the gauntlet of the hallway in slow motion. Nothing had changed. Willard is still passed out in his chair. I slowly put the gun up to his torso, muttered "Please let the gun fire," and then it happened. At 1:07 a.m. the gun fired, and a single hollow point .22 caliber bullet launched into Willard's chest.

The sound of the gun's detonation and the sight of the orange muzzle blast sent me running back to the kitchen where Veronica stood waiting. "Is he dead?" she asked. She then picked up the old rotary phone and dialed 911, telling the operator that she just shot her husband and needed an ambulance. After she made the call, Veronica went straight over to Holly Apartments. I was in shock. There I was stranded with Willard sitting in the chair with a gunshot wound to the chest that I had inflicted just moments earlier, and surprisingly no one was awakened by what had happened. Sammy, Sara, Jacob Lee, and my grandmother were still asleep. I was scared to death. All I could think to do was to jump back into bed with my granny and get as close to her as possible. My snuggling against her body woke her, and she asked why I was shaking and so clammy. I whispered, "I just shot Willard." "O my God, Mary, no," she responded.

I told my granny to be as quiet as possible because I was starting to hear moans from the living room where Willard was. Granny was having difficulty hearing the moans due to the blow she suffered just a day earlier. I told her that it sounded as though Willard was trying to get up from his chair. I heard the floor creaking with each step he took. My stomach cramped as I anticipated his walking into the room where I was. A few seconds later I heard a loud crash, the sound of Willard's falling to the floor. The relief I felt was overwhelming. At that moment I thought maybe everything was going to be okay and we all might survive the night. My life, as well as all our lives, forever changed from that time onward. What would happen to us, I wondered. I don't think that it occurred to me where I would go or what I would do afterward. I do remember my mother telling me, "Mary if you kill him, I will not have to go to jail." I guess that I imagined I would have a somewhat normal life and would never have to suffer abuse at the hands of Willard again, but the aftermath of the shooting would bring more instability and drama than I ever could have conceived.

When I heard an ambulance and police sirens, followed by someone's coming through the front door, I eased out of bed and walked toward the living room. Peeking around the corner, I saw medics cutting off Willard's shirt, his burgundy pants appearing wet with urine. I then watched them attempt to remove his boots and cut his pants off. There was no blood. I saw only a small wound on his upper chest. Everything seemed to be happening in slow motion. I wondered if anyone even noticed that I was standing there. Veronica and the police then came through the front door, walking past me straight into the kitchen where I had left the rifle. Moments later, a policeman who introduced himself as Officer Peeler asked whether he could talk to me outside. Before we made our way through the living room, paramedics had already taken Willard out the front door. He had an oxygen mask over his face, and they were trying to resuscitate him. I felt no sense of sadness, no remorse, no guilt. I was merely numb. Just as Officer Peeler began to question me, Veronica and another officer walked past us carrying the .22 rifle in a plastic bag. They went to his police car, where she began to tell her side of the story.

Officer Peeler asked me bluntly, "Who shot him?" "I did," I replied. "You're lying," he retorted. "No, I'm not," I replied. Officer Peeler said, "Then why did your mother call 911 and say she did it?" I responded saying, "I don't know, sir, but I am not lying to you."

Just then I slid my freezing hands into my pockets to warm them, and Officer Peeler exclaimed loudly, "Get your hands out of your pockets, now!" I was confused. When I told him that my hands were cold, he told me that he was going to check my hands for gunpowder residue. "Okay," I said, wondering how on earth he was going to do that.

At this juncture, Veronica changed her story about what had happened. She told another officer that she had nothing to do with this and that I committed the murder all on my own without any orders from her. Throughout this interrogation, Sammy, Sara, and Jacob Lee had remained fast asleep. My grandmother had gotten up and was sitting at the kitchen table. I never got a chance to talk to her. After Officer Peeler tested my hands for gunpowder residue, he walked me back into the house and asked where the cartridges were. I had no earthly idea. I thought that perhaps they were in the closet, where the rifle usually was sequestered. They were not there, and my effort to find them was fruitless. I then asked Officer Peeler whether I could wake up Sammy, thinking that he might know where the ammunition was because he had gotten into a lot of trouble for taking a loaded gun to school earlier that year.

As I walked into Sammy's room, he and Sara were sleeping soundly. Everything apparently had taken place without disturbing them. I wanted to tell Sammy that it was finally over, that we would never have to suffer the kind of pain Willard inflicted on us again. After I gently nudged Sammy a few times to awaken him, I told him that the police wanted to know where the shells for the rifle were. He sat up, looking a bit dazed, got up, walked into Veronica and Willard's bedroom, opened the top left drawer of the dresser, grabbed the box of Winchester hollow point bullets, and handed them to Officer Peeler. He then crawled back into bed and fell fast asleep. Looking back, I wonder why Sammy never questioned anything. Why did he go back to bed and never ask what was happening?

In the meantime, Veronica was still outside with the police officer finishing up her story regarding the events of that night. Officer Peeler walked through the house looking around, though I wasn't sure what he might have been searching for. By this time, several of the people living in Holly Apartments and a few other neighbors had started to gather outside to see what was going on. Shortly thereafter both officers got into their patrol cars and left. I then walked back outside and saw Veronica talking with some of the people that had gathered there. Veronica didn't even bother coming into the house; she told me that she was going over to a friend's apartment. I wasn't sure what to do myself. Walking back into the living room, I looked up at the clock; it was 2:25 a.m. Everyone was still sound asleep, except for my grandmother who was still sitting at the kitchen table. She was crying, so I hugged her and told her that I loved her very much and that we were going to be okay now. She wasn't sure how to respond. I imagine she knew something my young mind could not comprehend. I naively thought that it was all over because the police officers and everyone else had gone. I begin thinking about school, which was only a few hours away.

Returning to the living room, I noted that it was now 2:45 a.m. I wanted to lie down on the couch, feeling exhausted, and my mind was racing with all that had just taken place. I wondered why Veronica was with her friends across the road and not here with me. I was trying to imagine what would happen next when all of a sudden the telephone rang. I jumped up and ran to the kitchen, not wanting the ringing to awaken Jacob Lee. It was Veronica. She asked me if I would come over because she needed to talk about something. As I was walking out of the house, I looked back at the clock saying it was now 4:15 a.m. I realized then that I must have fallen asleep on the couch. Making my way across to Holly Apartments, I began to feel a little nervous, wondering what Veronica wanted to tell me. Maybe I had said something to Officer Peeler that upset her. If so, would she start beating me? The closer I drew to the apartment, the more hesitant I became.

When I knocked gently on the door, Debbie Fisher told me to come in and indicated that Veronica was in the bathroom. I found her sitting on the toilet with her hands to her head. When I asked her if she were okay, she looked up at me and said, "Willard's dead. He died this morning at 4:00 a.m." I wasn't particularly shocked since I thought that he was dead when he left the house. I just looked at Veronica... what did you expect? She began crying uncontrollably. "Isn't this what you wanted?" I asked. "You told me to kill him." I could not believe the way she was acting, and her behavior was exactly that. She was building a case for herself, though I didn't realize it at the time. I had become the enemy of Veronica Simms; she was out to save herself. Barely able to hold my eyes open, I sat down on Debbie's couch and fell fast asleep.

When I woke up, it was about eight o'clock in the morning, and Veronica was still there. She had a cup of coffee and had visibly calmed down from earlier. I told her that I was going back to the house to check on everyone, whereupon she said, "O my God. I need to see about the baby." Sammy and Sara were just starting to wake up, granny had already made coffee, and Jacob Lee was playing in his crib. While Veronica refilled her coffee cup, I changed Jacob Lee's urine soaked diaper and fed him a bottle. Sammy and Sara then came into the living room, they were dressed for school, and Sammy asked me whether we were going to school. I told him that I didn't think so. Veronica directed Sammy to sit on the couch because she needed to talk to him, while Sara went back to her room and started fiddling with her clothes. After Veronica disclosed that Willard had been shot and was dead, Sammy asked, "Who shot him?" I quietly said, "I did." Sammy showed no emotion, and I couldn't determine what he was feeling. He was, after all, only eight and Sara four. Because Sara would not have understood what had happened, Veronica didn't tell her. I was still holding Jacob Lee and asked Veronica to call Brother Jim. "Why?" she asked. I told her simply that I wanted to see him and begged her to please call.

Shortly after my request, a lady knocked on the front door. It was the local news crew wanting an interview. Veronica gladly let them in, and they asked her a few questions. Being very shy, I hardly even looked their way. A few minutes later Veronica said that they wanted to interview me for the evening news program. I didn't want to be interviewed, but Veronica insisted that I comply. So the crew set up their cameras and checked the lighting until they had me in just the right spot. I didn't want anybody at school to see me on television talking about how I had killed my stepfather, but I didn't have a choice. When Veronica told me to do something,

I had to do it or else. As the film crew was packing up, I began to wonder where Brother Jim was. When I asked Veronica again whether she had called him, she said, "Yes, I called him, and he said he would be over in a little while." In fact, I discovered later, she had not called him. A friend of Jim from Holly Apartments had contacted him and told him he needed to get over there. Jim had no idea what his friend was talking about until he said, "They killed Willard." Brother Jim immediately knew then what had happened.

Within minutes Brother Jim and Mrs. Kay pulled up in front of the old frame house while the news crew was still there. I had a sinking feeling, wondering what he thought of me. My God, I had killed someone, I realized. As the reality of what I had done settled into my brain. Brother Jim met me on the porch, gave me a big hug, and asked whether I was okay. We then walked back into the house and sat on the couch. "Am I going to hell for killing someone?" I inquired. "No, Mary, you're not going to hell." Pastor McCall then placed his arm around my shoulder and pulled me close to him. No one had ever shown me the kindness and love that he did. My heart longed for such fatherly affection. I wanted him to take me away from this place that I hated so much. I began to wonder what might ensue—whether we would remain in Adrian or move back to Cyclone with my grandmother. I was more confused now than ever before. Brother Jim said, "Let's walk out on the porch, Mary, and you can tell me what happened." So we sat down on an old couch, and I summarized the weekend leading up to the craziness. I told him that Veronica had asked me to shoot Willard and that I had done so. I also recounted the beatings and fighting, including my apprehension that Willard was going to make good on his threat to kill Veronica. Brother Jim then went back inside and asked Veronica if she had bruises. After she showed him her arms and back, he suggested we all go to the emergency room so that we would have a record of what had happened to us that weekend.

During the drive to the hospital, Sammy at one point said, "Mary, I hate you. You killed my Dad." For a moment there was dead silence. After a minute or so I said to Mrs. Kay, "This is all my fault." She gently responded, "Mary, it's not your fault. It's your mother and stepfather's fault for arguing, and his fault for drinking." I just sat there and hung my head, repeatedly saying, "I'm so sorry." It seemed as though we sat in the emergency room waiting room for hours before Veronica and I were called back. I was taken to a cold examination room where I was told to slip my clothes off, down to my underwear, while awaiting the doctor.

As I sat there, I was embarrassed by my shabby clothes and dirty socks, which I tried to hide under my pants.

I was always made fun of at school because I was poor. Just then a white coated man walked in and introduced himself as Dr. Roberts. He was a short man with thinning brown hair and wire framed glasses. I nodded my head in silent acknowledgment. Dr. Roberts confirmed that my name was Mary Butler and asked whether he could listen to my chest and back. I told him that would be fine. He then inquired about the bruises on my body. I told him bluntly that my stepfather Willard had hit me. I didn't go into any detail about what had happened to Willard since I wasn't sure whether or not he knew. I had never been to a doctor before, so I was eager to get dressed and go home.

After Dr. Roberts finished his examination and told me to get dressed, I returned to the waiting room where Brother Jim and I waited until Veronica came out. We didn't say much, mostly sitting in silence with occasional glances, smiles, and a wink or two. He made my heart so happy when he smiled or hugged me. A part of me knew that I had stolen his heart. I regarded Brother Jim as a father figure. Besides my grandfather, who had passed away years earlier, he was the only male in my life who had ever shown me any kind of positive attention and love. I wished so earnestly that he was my dad. I would have done anything to be his little girl. A short while later, Veronica emerged from her examination and we returned to the truck. When Brother Jim dropped us off in front of our house, he gave me a big hug, as he always did, and drove away. Veronica, as usual, headed across the road to Holly Apartments.

As Sammy walked around to the front of the house, I asked him where he was going. "Fishing," he said. "Do you want to go?" "No, I don't much feel like fishing," I replied. "Well, what do you want to do?" "I don't know, Sammy." Maybe he sensed that I was scared or nervous because he then asked me if I was going to get into trouble for shooting Willard. I told him that I didn't know. Inside the house, I queried my grandmother about what lay ahead, and she said that Veronica might have to go to jail for directing me to kill Willard. When I asked whether I might have to go to jail, she just shook her head. After hugging her, I went back outside to find Sammy and just as I was coming out the front door two police cars pulled up. I wanted to run, but I stood there completely frozen. It was Officer Peeler. "Where is your Mom?" he asked. "I am going to need you and her to come down to the police station with me." "Why? Are we going to jail?" "We need to get some statements about last night." "Okay. I'll get my mother."

I ran across to Holly Apartments. I told Veronica that a police officer was at the house and that he wanted us to go to the station to answer some questions. She didn't appear alarmed by the news. We walked back together and Officer Peeler asked us to get in the back seat of his cruiser. As we drove off, I saw Sammy standing outside watching us drive away. I thought I would be back soon, but I would never see that house again.

CHAPTER 8

Together Again

In the police station, I answered detailed questions about what happened on that fateful night of February 24, 1987. As the questions continued for what seemed like hours, I began to cry; the gravity of the situation finally dawning on me. After a short break, the interrogation resumed. Because it was now late afternoon, I started to worry about my grandmother and youngest brother. I knew that she was too frail to care for Jacob Lee, and Sammy could be difficult at times. Then there was little Sara. Where was she while all this was going on? Around four in the afternoon, a lady with red hair like mine came to see me, introducing herself as Ms. Janie. She told me that I would not be going back to the house in Adrian. When I asked her where I would be going, she said a foster home. She added that there was a nice lady in Weston, a small town over from where we were who took care of kids like me. When I asked whether my brothers and sisters would be going too, Ms. Janie answered that they would be accommodated at another foster home in Buckhannon. Since they were all biological brothers and sisters, they would be kept together. I started crying, and then wondered where my granny would go.

"Is my mother going to jail or something?" I asked next. "Yes. Veronica has been arrested," admitted Ms. Janie. "Why? She didn't do it. I did." "I know, Mary, but because you're so young she has to be held responsible for you." Nothing seemed to make sense. My life was getting worse by the minute. Who were these people I was going to live with, I asked myself, and would they like me? Then I began to wonder whether they knew what I had done. In short order, I was transported from the police department to a lawyer's office, where I sat for three hours. It was starting to get dark outside, and the darker it got the more frightened I became. I had nothing but the clothes on my back. I felt completely helpless. Perhaps if I could call Brother Jim, I thought, he could come to get me and take me home with him. As time passed, Ms. Janie, the social worker, came out to the waiting area and asked me if I was ready to leave. Tired of sitting, I told her I was but inquired whether I could go to Brother Jim's house instead of a foster home in Weston. She said that was not possible because I was in the state's custody now and had to be placed in a foster residence. I remember thinking that I had no idea what all this meant, but I had no other choice. Half an hour later, at age eleven, I entered the foster care system. I was terrified of the unknown but wanted to believe that the future would be better than the life I had been living.

Late on the evening of February 25, 1987, I arrived at the home of Jill and Thomas Ridgeway. I was greeted at the door by Mrs. Ridgeway, a tall and slim lady with a kind smile. She invited me in and asked my name. When I told her, she said that she had seen me earlier on TV and immediately had said to herself, "I hope that little girl gets to come here." I felt a sense of comfort and relief, as though she already knew me. Mrs. Ridgeway then offered me some chocolate cake that she said she had made especially for me when she learned that I would be coming to her home. She told me I could have as much as I wanted. I ate two delicious pieces, the first food I had eaten in three days. Again I experienced a sense of comfort. There were several children at the home, three of whom were her biological children and six others who were foster kids like me. Ms. Janie stayed with me for a short while to make sure I was alright. Upon leaving she gave me a big hug and told me she would be in touch soon.

That night I went to bed on a small cot in a room with two other girls. When I told Mrs. Ridgeway that

I was afraid, she asked, "Of what?" I replied that I was afraid of Willard coming to kill me. Mrs. Ridgeway patiently reassured me that I had nothing to worry about because Willard was dead and never could hurt me again. I wanted to believe her, and I guess that part of me did, but I couldn't get him out of my mind. She wished me goodnight and plugged in a night light. As I laid there I began to cry, having always slept with my grandmother who made me feel safe. I wondered what she was doing, and I missed my brothers and sisters.

The next day all the kids were getting ready for school when I woke up. Mrs. Ridgeway was rushing around making sure that everybody had eaten breakfast and had their book bags. While they were leaving to catch the bus, she asked me if I would like some Coco Wheat. Although I had no idea what it was, I ate the cereal as fast as I could because I was so hungry. When I queried Mrs. Ridgeway about when I would be able to go to school, she said that she didn't know yet but that as soon as she found out something she would tell me. As time passed, I was not allowed to go back to Buckhannon to see my brothers and sisters. Worse than that, I couldn't see Brother Jim. I wasn't even permitted to return to school to finish sixth grade. Instead, I stayed home all day with Mrs. Ridgeway for the rest of the school year, although I received a couple of school books and did some independent work. Unfortunately, I had a lot of recurrent nightmares about what had happened. In these nightmares, I imagined Willard walking toward me, and I would awaken screaming in fear. I also started thinking that Willard's family members were outside looking for me because they wanted to kill me for what I had done. Thus, it wasn't long until I was told that I had to start going to see a psychiatrist named Dr. Lipski. I met with him every week, for almost a year and we talked about the night I shot Willard. Dr. Lipski asked lots of questions about my childhood, usually letting me do all the talking. I now realize that this regimen was very therapeutic, giving me an outlet to express my emotions and frustrations. However, it took Dr. Lipski a long time to convince me that what had happened wasn't my fault. For a very long time I blamed myself, and I'm sure it was difficult for him to make me see things from another point of view.

After about six months of living with the Ridgeway's, I was told that I had to live with another foster family in Beckley. I was confused as to why I had to leave. I finally was in a place where I felt comfortable and where no one was hurting me, but the social worker told me that due to the publicity surrounding Willard's death the case was becoming very high-profile. For my safety, I needed to move farther away from that area. The trial had yet to start, and I had not been allowed to see or speak to Veronica. I assumed she was in jail. I later found out that she spent four months in jail and was released on bond until the trial. A few days thereafter I got some good news. I was told that Sammy, Sara, and Jacob Lee would also be coming to Beckley and that we would all be staying with the same family. I couldn't wait to pack up my stuff and go. A week later we loaded up for the three-hour drive, I was traveling with one social worker while my siblings were with another. The environment in Beckley was quite different in that there were no other foster children. The young couple with whom we lived, David and Carolyn Shoobie, had only one small daughter named Gracie who was less than a year old at the time. I immediately fell in love with the family and shared a room with my sister and Gracie.

It was here that I learned about responsibility. The Schoobie's had a very structured way of doing things. All of us were put on a "level" system, which meant that our behavior, completion of chores, and other responsibilities determined our extracurricular activities. For example, at level one we could spend as much time outside as we wanted. At level two, we could spend only a maximum of two hours outdoors. Lastly, at level three we were entitled to no time outside. In addition, there was an incentive program that entailed a monetary reward for each level achieved. For me, this proved an easy and valuable structure. I felt such deep gratitude to the people who had taken me into their homes that I wanted to do whatever I could to make them happy with me. I probably believed that, if I could get them to love me, then maybe they would keep me. For Sammy, however, this program proved quite difficult. He had a temper, never wanted to do his chores, and often would talk back insolently. I tried many times to tell him that, if he would just do what the Schoobie's asked, he could play outside and earn more money. Our foster parents in Beckley had several mason jars with our names on them. Every morning when we came downstairs there would be fake money on top of the jars, more or less depending on the level reached on the preceding day. Once we saved up our money, we could buy things. The first item I ever bought was a Spud Mackenzie skateboard. I then saved up enough to purchase a fuchsia colored freestyle bike. For me, the reward system was an excellent way to learn responsibility, but for Sammy it was more than he could endure.

I spent a little over a year with the Schoobie's, completing seventh grade in Beckley, West Virginia. During my time there they encouraged me to sign up for softball. I was very much a tomboy and loved sports. This was the first time that anyone had ever encouraged me to get involved with anything. I was a quick learner, and the coach who liked me asked whether I would be the pitcher. Our team was called the Roadrunners, and we were much like the "Bad News Bears." Although we weren't very good, I made the All-star team that year. I was so excited to be recognized for doing something well. I also liked football, which David, Sammy, and I sometimes played in the yard. When I asked David whether I could sign up for football, he said "Sure." Although I was the only girl on the team and weighed about seventy-five pounds, I wasn't afraid of anybody or anything. During seventh grade, I was a wide receiver for the Trap Hill Wildcats. Much to my regret, given many positive experiences while under their care, my time with the Schoobie's would soon end. The following summer brought more changes for my siblings and I. Sammy, Sara, and Jacob Lee went back to their original foster home because the family that had been taking care of them right after the shooting wanted to adopt them. They left that summer to live with their new parents. I continued with the Schoobie's for a few more weeks until the start of Veronica's murder trial, at which time I returned to the home of Jill and Thomas Ridgeway, my original foster parents. I never stopped wishing that I could be adopted by Jim and Kay McCall, but the social workers would not allow me to see anybody from Upshur County prior to the trial.

CHAPTER 9

The Trial

With the trial date looming, I often found myself thinking more and more about my estranged family wondering where they were living and how they were doing. I was not allowed to have any contact with them after the shooting. It was as though I had been cut off from the only family I knew, made to accept the fact that I had become a foster child in the blink of an eye Or, in my case with the pull of a trigger. The trial was set to start on June 15, 1988, and my therapist, Dr. Lipski, informed me that the judge had agreed to allow me to testify in the case. I was extremely nervous about being called to the stand, but Dr. Lipski told me to just tell the truth about what happened that night and everything would be alright. While I was busy settling into life with the Ridgeway's, the prosecution and defense attorneys were busy preparing for a trial like few others.

Because Veronica could not afford to pay for legal representation, the court appointed two local attorneys to represent her in the case. She had been charged with first-degree murder, to which she entered a plea of not guilty. Her defense team would argue that Willard was shot in self-defense and if he had not been shot that early February morning, he would have killed Veronica when he got up from his drunken slumber. Of course, this was unlike other such cases because Veronica had recruited her minor daughter to commit the crime. Both the prosecution and defense would diligently call their witnesses to the stand and get right to the heart of the matter. The crucial question was whether Veronica's orders for her daughter, a minor, to kill Willard Simms constituted self-defense or first-degree murder as charged.

The honorable Judge James Coolie was scheduled to preside over the trial, which would involve about twenty-five witnesses and seven full days of testimony before the prosecution would rest its case against Veronica Simms. Judge Coolie made it clear to the defense team that the only verdicts they would be allowed to return in this case would be: not guilty, guilty of first-degree murder, guilty of second-degree murder, and first-degree murder with the recommendation of mercy at sentencing. The last of the three guilty verdicts would allow Veronica to be eligible for parole after serving a minimum of ten years in the state prison. The trial got started as scheduled, nearly sixteen months after the shooting. The small courthouse in rural Buckhannon, West Virginia, found itself in the middle of a media frenzy. Everybody in Upshur and surrounding counties were interested in the trial's outcome. On the first day when I arrived at the courthouse, the media presence was overwhelming. Reporters and photographers were everywhere. The social worker I was riding with told me to cover my face with a newspaper when we passed by the photographers. She pulled her car into a narrow alley at the rear of the courthouse where two sheriff's deputies awaited my arrival. When we pulled up, they quickly opened the car door and assisted me in the courthouse. They then escorted me straight into the Judge's chambers where they left me in dread of what was to come.

While I was required to be at the courthouse every day during the trial, I was never allowed to be in the same room with other witnesses or in the courtroom where the trial was being conducted. As I sat in the judge's chambers on the first day, I noticed all the family pictures on his bookcase and found myself thinking of what it must be like to be a judge's daughter and to have a normal family life. I then remembered Brother Jim and Mrs. Kay and began to cry. The moment was interrupted by the social worker entering and asking me if everything was okay. She told me that the trial was about to begin and that the judge had requested my appearance in the courtroom for the swearing-in oath. This would be the first time I had an opportunity to see Veronica in over a year. When I entered the packed court room for the first time, I saw Veronica sitting at a table with two men dressed in suits sitting on each side of her. I was correct in my assumption that these men were her court appointed attorneys. She made eye contact with me but showed no emotion, not even a smile. She was dressed in a black dress with a white floral overlay and looked to be in good health. I reflected briefly on what the past year had been like for her while awaiting trial. I would soon learn that she had made bail and been released from the county jail after spending several months there.

For the past nine months, she had been living in Clarksburg, West Virginia with my grandmother. Clarksburg was about one hour's drive north of the small town where I had been living in foster care for the past year. Judge Coolie then called for order and started the proceeding. After Judge Coolie gave pretrial instructions to the jurors, he informed them that they would be going for a jury view of the house in Adrian where Willard had been shot. He had arranged for deputies to drive jurors to the house where they would be examining the scene, which had been undisturbed since the shooting. I would be sworn in with a large group of witnesses prior to the jurors' being dismissed for the trip. After the swearing-in, Veronica, Judge Coolie, the attorneys, and all the jurors left for the view while I was taken back to the judge's chambers once again to await the call for me to take the stand. When the group returned, the defense and prosecution started the trial with their opening statements. The prosecution presented a forty-five minute statement that highlighted the evidence they would be introducing and reiterated the Judge's pretrial instructions on what verdicts the jury could return. The prosecutor told the jury, "The case you will hear might be like none other in the history of the world, a case where the defendant used her own daughter to commit the crime and then turned around and claimed self-defense to escape punishment." Although opening statements were just a preview of the upcoming trial, the jury was probably beginning to feel as though this was an open-and-shut case, but the defense soon had time to make its case to the jury as well. The defense attorney told jurors Veronica's side of the story; how she, her mother, and her children were all victims of abuse and mental torture at the hands of Willard Simms. The defense team went into detail about the abuse and Willard's mistreatment of my grandmother. They pledged to call reliable witnesses to the stand who would attest to the abuse they had seen over the years. What seemed to be a slam-dunk case for the prosecution would prove to be self-defense as substantiated by the battered woman syndrome.

After the opening statements were completed, the judge ordered a recess and informed everyone that after lunch the prosecutor would begin to call witnesses to the stand. I would be one of the first witnesses to be called to testify. Although the entire trial was recorded on VHS, the judge ordered the recording device to be turned off during my testimony, probably because I was a minor. I nervously kept thinking about what my counselor, Dr. Lipski had told me: "Just tell the truth, and everything will be fine." The questions about Willard's behavior made me relive my horrific past, and I thought that the questioning would never end. I simply told the truth as best I could remember. The prosecution would be the first to question me about the events that transpired that early February morning. As the questions started coming my way, I found myself feeling sorry for Veronica. I knew that what she had done was wrong, but I also knew what she and my family had endured at the hands of Willard Simms. As my soft childish voice answered the prosecutor's questions, Veronica just sat at the defense table with a blank stare on her face. As I answered the questions, I remember recalling my therapist's words again: "just tell the truth and everything will be fine." I found it difficult to relive the events of February 24, 1987, but I knew I had to tell the story and be truthful in my words. The lead prosecutor's line of questioning was centered on the shooting itself. He kept asking me about the gun and how many times I had gone into the living room to shoot Willard. He also asked me what Veronica was doing while I was walking through the house with the rifle in hand. I felt as though I was answering the same questions over and over again. At last, the prosecutor said, "No further questions, your honor," and I felt a huge sense of relief. Then the judge asked the defense attorney, "Do you have any questions for the witness? I felt sick when he responded, "Yes, your honor we have a few questions for this witness."

The defense attorney's questions were more about violence and abuse we had suffered at the hands of Willard Simms. I remember the renewed sense of anger I felt toward Willard as I told the jury about the abuse he had inflicted against me and my grandmother; all the times he had terrorized us with his western style pistol, the names he would call us, the physical and mental abuse he would hand down. I had to talk about every thing we had endured at the hands of this man, and at times, I found myself thinking that Veronica should be exonerated of the murder charge and set free. My total time on the stand was just under an hour. This was the only time I would be called to testify during the seven day trial, but much more testimony by others soon followed.

The next witness called to the stand would be Officer John Russell, the primary investigating officer. Officer Russell was the first responding officer to the 911 call after the shooting. He told the lead prosecutor that he had received the radio call at 12:47 a.m. and picked up a State Conservation Officer by the name of Steve Long on his way to the scene. Officer Russell knew Willard and Veronica from past disturbances and was familiar with the area as well as the residence where the 911 call had come from. Officer Russell described the scene when he arrived at the house where the shooting had occurred. "Mr. Simms was lying flat on his back in the living room when I entered the house," the officer stated. "He was in a semi conscientious state but was able to tell me that he had been shot in the chest. He did not know who had shot him but he kept saying, 'I'm going to die, I'm going to die.'" Officer Russell told the court that he began to administer first aid to Mr. Simms as soon as they arrived at the scene. He described a small puncture wound he had discovered after removing the maroon colored western style shirt and a basic white t-shirt. "The puncture wound was located in the upper right quadrant of the victim's chest. There was very little blood coming from the wound when I was administering first aid," the officer stated. While Officer Russell administered first aid to Willard another police officer, officer Peeler, arrived, began gathering evidence, and interviewing suspects and witnesses. Shortly after the paramedics arrived on the scene, Willard was readied for transport and taken to the local hospital in Buckhannon, West Virginia, for treatment of a gunshot wound to the chest. Officer Russell stated, "I remember Mr. Simms saying to the paramedics, 'don't let me die; don't let me die' as they were loading him in the back of the ambulance." Officer Russell would accompany Willard during transport to the hospital in hopes to get more information about what had happened but Willard would slip into unconscious during transport and never tell the officer who had shot him.

The emergency room doctors quickly determined that the gunshot wound Willard suffered would require advanced surgery to stop the internal bleeding and that he would need to be Medivacked to West Virginia University Medical Center in Morgantown, West Virginia, for the surgery. "After Mr. Simms was taken to the helicopter pad, I returned back to the scene and continued my investigation," Officer Russell stated. When he returned to the scene, Officer Russell had collected items of evidence to include: the two shirts that had been removed from Willard's body at the scene, one bolt action "Savage Stevens" brand twenty-two caliber rifle with scope, one partial box of twenty-two caliber Winchester shells, one spent Winchester Super X shell casing, one small piece of paper found in Willard's shirt pocket with the name "John Bowman" scribed in Willard's handwriting with an address and phone number for the man. John Bowman was the man who had wrecked the jeep a few days prior to the shooting. As the items were introduced into evidence, the lead prosecutor would dust his hands tidily as if the items were tainted with evil. While Veronica's defense team would cross-examine Officer Russell, they would fail to discount his investigation techniques or his crime scene findings.

The next witness the prosecution called to the stand would be Dr. Frank Kilman. Dr. Kilman was the Forensic Pathologist who completed the autopsy of Willard Simms' corpse to determine the cause of death. Dr. Kilman described the projectile's path of destruction that resulted in Willard's death. Through his testimony, it was clear that the bullet had struck an artery in his abdominal area and caused a massive amount of internal bleeding. The sole reason for his testimony was obvious; to show the jury that Willard Simms had indeed died of the gunshot wound he received the early morning hours of February 24, 1987. The defense team asked Dr. Kilman about other body marking, specifically if Willard had and any tattoos. The doctor went on to describe two tattoos he had noted during the autopsy saying, "Mr. Simms had one nonprofessional tattoo on his right arm of a heart with an arrow going through it and a light blue in color and a 7.5 nonprofessional tattoo of a naked woman on his left arm, both were light blue ink and nonprofessional." The relevance of the questions the defense team asked was not questioned by the prosecution and the doctor was dismissed without further questioning.

Next to take the stand was Officer Peeler. Officer Peeler completed the first interview with both me and Veronica after the shooting. He would read to the jury the initial statement that Veronica had given at 1:15 a.m. the morning of the shooting. The initial interview would be conducted in Officer Peeler's police cruiser. Veronica would be seated in the back seat of the patrol car and Officer Peeler and Conservation Officer Long would be seated in the front seat during the interview. After reading Veronica her rights, she would start the process of clearing herself of any wrongdoing and put me solely responsible for the shooting. "Mary shot him while I was asleep" was her first words spoken. The initial statement given by Veronica indicated that she was fast asleep on the loveseat in the living room when she was awakened by the sound of the gun firing just a few feet from where she slept. "Mary went into my bedroom closet and got the gun while I was asleep on the loveseat. The sound of the gun firing scared me to death," she told the officer in her initial statement. After giving her initial statement Officer Peeler got out of the car to confer with Officer Russell prior to leaving the scene in the ambulance.

At this time, Veronica and Conservation Officer Long were left alone in the patrol car. Veronica had more to say but Officer Long advised her to hold her thought until Officer Peeler got back in the car. Before he could tell her to hold her thoughts, she said: "I didn't shoot Willard, but I guess I'm responsible." I guess she knew that I would be telling the police my side of the story and our stories would be as different as night and day. After Officer Peeler completed his testimony, the prosecution called Conservation Officer Long to the stand for his testimony concerning Veronica's statement she had made in the absence of Officer Peeler. The defense would have no questions for either officer and the first day of court was complete. The days to follow would bring more startling revelations about the truth behind the sinister lifestyle, physical abuse, mental torture, and ultimately the shooting that ended one nightmare and started another.

The second day of the trial would bring testimony from many residents of the small village of Adrian. The prosecution called several witnesses that had spoken to both Veronica and myself shortly after the shooting. One witness would state that Veronica had initially stated that she had shot Willard herself but this story would change within a few hours when she would state that "Mary was the one that shot him." The witness would go on to say that Veronica would also say, "I can't believe she shot him." This same witness would also testify that she had talked to me after the shooting and that I had admitted to her and several other people that I had shot Willard and had stated that "I hoped he dies". While I don't recall these exact words, I'm sure that this is how I felt, I wanted so desperately for it all to be over. Veronica had convinced me that killing Willard would set us free from the life of abuse we had come to know. The next witness to be called to the stand would be Joan Anderson, a resident of Holly Apartments and a close friend of Veronica.

Joan's testimony would reveal that Willard was seldom home due to his occupation. "When he took the truck driving job, he was only home every other weekend," she told the jury. Joan would go on to testify that Veronica would stay at the apartments much of the time when her husband was out of town working. She also indicated that there were no physical signs of abuse but that Veronica had told her that Willard would hit her from time to time. Joan also testified to the story that Veronica had told her just after the shooting. "I shot him, I meant to do it, and I hope the he dies," Veronica told Joan after Willard was rushed away in the ambulance.

She also testified that Veronica would refuse to take calls from the hospital the night of the shooting and that she was the one that had to tell Veronica that Willard had died in surgery at around four in the morning. When word came of Willard's death Joan testified that Veronica went hysterical. Veronica started screaming, "I loved him, I loved him, and I didn't want him to die." Joan would also testify that by daybreak the story had changed and that now Veronica was claiming that her eleven-year-old daughter had shot Willard while she was asleep. Joan had told Veronica, "you better get your act together fast because the police will be coming back soon." Joan would be correct in her assumption and the next person to be called to the stand to testify would be the arresting officer, Upshur County Sheriff Fred Gladden.

Sheriff Gladden would take the stand and testify that he and another officer had driven out to Adrian Wednesday afternoon to get another statement from both myself and Veronica. "After interviewing both Mary and Veronica at the crime scene the afternoon of the twenty-fifth, I decided to take both of them to the sheriff's office in Buckhannon to complete a subsequent interview and get a formal statement from both Mary and Veronica." Sheriff Gladden would go on to read the Question and Answer interview he had conducted on February 25, 1987. During this question and answer interview, it was obvious that what had happened the night before had been exerting a heavy toll on Veronica's conscientiousness. "She came clean during the subsequent interview and told me every detail of the shooting," the sheriff would testify. Veronica had admitted to recruiting me to shoot her husband. She had also admitted to the gun failing to fire on the first two attempts and she had admitted that she was awake and actively orchestrating the entire chain of events that led up to the shooting of her husband. With my sworn testimony and the admission of guilt by Veronica, the prosecution had a strong case against her but the defense team would attempt to show that the murder was justified by the fear of Willard Simms and the potential for violence base on a horrific past and the very threats he had made against her just before passing out the evening he was shot. The next witness to take the stand would have firsthand knowledge of the extent of injury that Willard had sustained as a result of the shooting.

The prosecution would now call Dr. Richard Latimore to the stand. Dr. Latimore was the emergency room physician that was on call the evening of the shooting. He testifies that he had given initial emergency care to Willard Simms upon arrival to St. Joseph's Hospital in Buckhannon. He stated that Mr. Simms had arrived at the hospital at around 1:45 a.m. and was in a semi conscientious state upon arrival. Dr. Latamore testified that Willard was given a blood transfusion and glucose to stabilize him for transport to WVU Medical Center by helicopter. The doctor would go on to say "during the course of treatment, Mr. Simms did stabilize a bit but was mostly unresponsive during treatment. Mr. Simms did, however, respond to the chest tube being inserted by saying "just let me die – just let me die." The doctor would testify that Willard would be medivacked to WVU Medical Center after spending approximately forty minutes at St. Joseph's Hospital. After Dr.

Latimore's testimony ended, the defense team would move to enter a motion for a lesser charge. The judge would explain the situation to the jurors and excuse them from the court room during the in suing debate.

The defense team would ask Judge Coolie to consider a motion to eliminate both first and second degree murder as possible verdicts that could be rendered in the case. They stated that the prosecution had failed to establish premeditation or malice in the case, but Judge Coolie quickly denied the motion citing that my testimony and the testimony of Dr. Kilman as "strong evidence to support the existing charge of first degree murder." While the defense was looking for a lesser charge, they would be forced to prove that Veronica's actions were justified and that the only way out of the situation was to kill her husband. This would prove to be a difficult task for the defense team, but they had many witnesses aligned to support the notion that Veronica was the victim in this case and that she had no way out other than to kill Willard Simms.

Day three of the trial would bring the defense witnesses to the stand. The first witness to be called for the defense was Mr. Albertson; he was their landlord for a short period of time. He was a very credible witness for the defense and was clearly telling the truth about what had happened to Veronica while living in the small rental camper in Cox Mills. The defense team also called Mr. Albertson's daughter to the stand to attest that she too had witnessed markings on Veronica's body to indicate that Veronica had been abused while living in her dad's camper trailer. While the testimony was compelling and needed to be told, the prosecution made light of the testimony by asking how many times they actually saw Willard abusing Veronica. Neither witness had actually seen Willard strike her nor was the number of incidents they could recall limited to the one occasion. The next witness to be called by the defense team would be an attorney that Veronica had met with, in 1985, when she was contemplating leaving her husband.

The attorney testified that Veronica had in fact came into his office and inquired about getting an absolute divorce in March 1985. He testified that she had sited physical abuse as the reason for seeking a divorce. "Home life with Willard was tough sometimes," Veronica told the attorney during the 1985 meeting. The consultation would end with the attorney informing Veronica of a five hundred dollar retainer fee that would need to be paid in full to proceed with filing a motion for divorce. Needless to say, Veronica had no money and was unable to raise the retainer fee. She would return to the life of abuse that she had learned to live with. The attorney would go on to testify that Veronica had called his office again in October of the same year requesting a title search on a property in Frenchton that she and her husband Willard were considering purchasing. This opened the door for the prosecution to claim that the couple had reconciled the marriage and the abuse had ended. "After all, what couple contemplating divorce is looking to purchase property together?" the lead prosecutor would ask during cross-examination of the witness. Instead of helping the defense, the testimony actually hurt the case they were attempting to build for Veronica Simms. However, the next witness to be called by the defense team would provide a credible pattern of violence from Willard Simms, his ex-wife, Susan Kidman.

Mrs. Kidman testified that Willard had called her a few days before the shooting and asked her if she could keep the children until he could find another job. As I watched the trial footage, I got the sense that Willard was once again threatening to take Veronica's children and strip her of her only means of survival (the welfare check and food stamps that came with having four children and no job). Susan would refuse to keep the children stating that one of her own children had been ill and the burden of four more kids to care for was too great. She would also state that Willard never abused her or their two daughters but this testimony would be proven untrue by the defense team's cross-examination. The defense would insist that Susan was still angry with Veronica due to the adulteress affair that destroyed her marriage in 1979. After all, Veronica was pregnant with Willard's child at the time and the affair would lead to the eventual break up of Willard and Susan. She would testify that Willard was a good husband and a supportive father but the defense would argue differently. "Mrs. Kidman, did you ever file the nonsupport order against Mr. Simms in 1979?" the defense attorney asked. She would answer no. "What about 1980 or 1981?" Once again she would answer no but would go on to say that the Welfare Department handled nonsupport matters and that she received welfare checks to support the two minor children and food stamps to feed them. The defense would continue to challenge Susan's testimony that Willard was never abusive to her during their four year marriage. "Mrs., Kidman, have you ever swore a warrant against Mr. Simms?" the defense team asked. Susan answered, "No, never." "Are you sure about that Mrs. Kidman?" he would ask. "Yes, I'm sure about that" Susan answered. But this answer would prove to be untrue when the defense introduced an Assault and Battery Warrant filed in 1978. The lead prosecutor erupted; "Objection your

Honor, we know nothing about this piece of evidence the defense is introducing." Judge Coolie ordered the document to be shown to the prosecutor and the cross-examination continued. "Do you recognize this document?" the defense asks. "Yes – I guess so, but nothing ever became of it" Susan stated. "Would you please read the complaint to the jury," the defense attorney asked. In a soft voice, she read the complaint aloud, "He threatened to beat the life out of me if I did not do everything he told me to do." "So Willard was a good husband and a good father to you and your children," the defense would ask. "I guess so," Susan would reply. "No further questions for this witness your honor," the attorney would state. Susan's testimony would show a clear history of abusive behavior by Willard Simms and would leave the jurors with a better sense of how life must have been while living in his presence.

The defense team would continue to make their case by calling many of the residents from Holly Apartments to testify about Willard's behavior and the lifestyle Veronica had grown to accept while living in Adrian. As each resident would testify, the same story would come from each witness from the apartments; sex, drinking, and fighting were a part of life at Holly Apartments. Most would testify that Willard was gone most of the time and that Veronica's behavior would change drastically whenever he came in from work. "Whenever he was working, she would spend a lot of time at the apartments hanging out with her friends and having a good time," several witnesses would state. Many residents had witnessed Veronica and Willard fighting on numerous occasions prior to the shooting and several testified that they saw bruises on Veronica's body several times during the two years the couple lived in Adrian. For each witness the defense would call to testify that Willard was an abusive husband, the prosecution would paint Veronica as a promiscuous alcoholic that only wanted to party and have sex with other men while her husband was away working. The defense team would end the barrage of witnesses who were residents of Holly apartments with testimony by Ben Jones.

Ben Jones was the last person, aside from the family, that had seen Willard the evening that lead to the shooting. Mr. Jones had been pressured by Willard the entire weekend to tell him about Veronica's behavior when he was away working. Mr. Jones testified that by eleven in the evening on the night of the shooting, Willard was very drunk and used the word "belligerent" to describe his state of mind. "He was just sitting on the porch step staring down at the ground," Jones would say. He went on to say that at half past eleven; Willard staggered into the house and sat down in a chair in the living room where he had been shot. "After he sat down in the chair, his head slumped toward his chest and it appeared to me that he passed out. After I saw him pass out, I left and went back across the road to the apartments," Jones testified. "After a few minutes passed, I heard the sound of a gunshot and knew something bad had happened over the Simms's place," he said in closing. While Mr. Jones' testimony did reveal the drunken state of Willard the evening of the shooting, the prosecutor would again use this witness to show that Veronica was a promiscuous party girl when her husband was away. Mr. Jones even testified that Veronica would flirt with him when she was at the apartments and that he had seen John Bowman hanging out with Veronica on more than one occasion. While the prosecution would do a good job of showing Veronica as an unfaithful wife and an irresponsible mother, Mr. Jones's testimony would support the claim that Willard was drunk and somewhat out of control the night he was shot. The defense would continue calling witnesses to support that Veronica had suffered from battered woman syndrome prior to the shooting and the evidence presented seemed to support this claim.

The defense team called numerous doctors, counselors and social workers to the stand to prove that Veronica was the victim in this case and that Willard's death was a justified means to end the abuse. After the shooting, the defense team arranged for Veronica to meet with an expert in family counseling. She would meet with the doctor twice and through verbal interviews, the doctor determined that Veronica did indeed suffer from battered woman syndrome. Through the testimony of these professional witnesses, it was clear that Veronica and Willard had some major marital problems and that the problems had been in existence for many years leading up to the shooting. It also revealed that Willard and Veronica had been through formal counseling in 1983 and 1984. Records also supported that Willard had been seen in March 1983 at the Summit Center in Glenville, West Virginia. The Center Director, Don Williamson, would testify that Willard had admitted having problems with alcohol and was prone to abuse it. The prosecution would dismiss this as "episodic use", but it was clear that a serious problem was present when Willard showed up at the Summit Center impaired. Mr. Williamson went on to testify that he had met with Veronica and Willard as a couple in April 1983 to discuss the problems they were having at home. "The first time we met, I separated them for general discussion and this was when Mrs. Simms showed me bruises she claimed to have received from spousal abuse. I informed her of the Domestic Violence Shelter here in town and urged her to consider leaving Mr. Simms if the abuse continues." He testified that during the second meeting Willard became loud, boisterous, and angrily walked out on the session. "I once again urged Mrs. Simms to seek relief through the Women's Shelter and she said she would think about it," said Williamson. While the defense team focused on the marriage counseling portion of Mr. Williamson's testimony, the prosecution had additional Summit Center records that would call questions to Veronica's parenting skills.

According to Summit Center Records, Veronica had met with family counselors on numerous occasions in 1984 to discuss the difficulties she was having with her children. "Veronica and her children would attend two Parent Skill Improvement Workshops at the Center before dropping out," Mr. Williamson told the court. He would go on to say that "the center felt that more help was needed for the Simms family and that the family seemed to be a bit dysfunctional." As if this was not bad enough, Veronica would also express a lack of care for her oldest son Sammy and told one counselor that "she could not think of one thing she liked about Sammy." This statement would lead to more extensive counseling sessions that would focus on her parenting skills and attempt to improve her relationship with Sammy as well as the other children living in her care. When I heard this testimony, I couldn't help but to think about how much Sammy looked like Willard. Even at an early age, Sammy looked and acted a lot like Willard. Perhaps when Veronica looked at Sammy all she could see was his dad, the man who had made her life a complete nightmare. Against the advice of professional counselors, Veronica would abandon the counseling sessions in the fall of 1984. The final entries in the Summit Center Records would conclude that "Veronica lacked essential parenting skills, lacked self-confidence, and had very little family support." According to the records, Veronica would never return to the Summit Center for help, but an anonymous report of child abuse less than a year later would bring another attempt for intervention from the Department of Social Services.

The defense team called a social worker, Mrs. Janie, to testify about what she had found during her investigation. She testified that someone outside the family had called DSS and reported both abuse and neglect of the Simms children in 1985. Mrs. Janie would visit the Simms home twice in September 1985 to interview Veronica and Willard as well as their children. Mrs. Janie testified that during the first visit, Sammy was very "loud and boisterous" the entire time she was at the home. As a result of the investigation, DSS had advised Veronica that she should consider attending a parenting workshop, but no other action would be taken. She went on to testify that Willard had called her in late October of the same year to discuss child care options for his children. This would have been the time frame when Veronica had moved to Cyclone with Dean Williams and Willard had come and taken the kids and what little money Veronica had taken when she left Frenchton. With Mrs. Janie's testimony completed, the defense team then called on the immediate family to convince the jury of what a monster Willard Simms was behind closed doors. The next witness the defense brought the most emotional testimony of all witnesses. Someone who is very near and dear to my heart; my seventy-six-year-old grandmother. As I watched the video of my granny's testimony for the first time, I experienced a wave of intense emotions. It had been nearly twenty-three years since I last saw her sweet face or heard her precious voice. The happiness I felt at first sight of her quickly turned to pain as I began to realize what all she had gone through in her advanced age. Anger soon replaced the pain I was feeling as she began to tell the jury about the mental & physical abuse she had endured at the hands of Willard Simms.

The defense team would be the first to question my granny. The first thing that got my attention when I watched her testimony was the fact that she was hard of hearing in her right ear. As the attorney would ask her questions, she would turn her head so that her good ear would pick up his voice. I quickly remembered that Willard had struck her in the ear the day before I shot him and the defense team would be quick to point out that very fact. In an elevated voice, the attorney would ask her about her hearing problem. "Mrs. Butler, why are you having problems hearing me through your right ear?" In her elderly, frail voice, she would reply with a simple explanation "Willard hit me in the side of the head." "Mrs. Butler, did Willard ever hit Veronica?" the attorney would ask. "Yes – all the time," she replied. "What about the children, did he ever hit them?" asked the attorney. "Yes – Willard was mean to those kids," she replied. As I watched my granny testify to all that she had gone through, tears begin to fill my eyes and I would soon find myself feeling enraged at both Veronica and Willard. They had put my granny through complete torture for their own selfish reasons. Had it not been for her social security check, they would have never brought her back to Adrian. She would go on to testify that Willard at times would point guns at her and other family members and that on one occasion he had fired the gun in the air while holding her hostage. "Willard was mean and hateful to all of us," she said in closing. My grandmother was a powerful witness for the defense and the prosecution had a hard time discounting her testimony. The next witness to take the stand was easy prey for the prosecution; next to be called was the defendant in the case, Veronica Simms herself.

The decision to put Veronica on the stand was a strategic move by the defense team. With my grandmother's compelling testimony now on record, and all the other testimony that was completed prior to this point of the trial, all that Veronica's defense team could hope for was that the jury would feel sorry for her and give her the lesser of the three verdicts. A finding of "not guilty" was highly unlikely and the defense team knew this going into the trial. Veronica would take the stand in her own defense on June 18, 1988. It was obvious that the defense wanted to paint Veronica as a victim of years of abuse and that the shooting was justified based on her fear of her husband. They would ask her to recall her entire past starting with the first time she ever met Willard. They would show the jury that she was an uneducated woman with only an eighth grade education and that she indeed had relied on welfare for survival. The defense team asked Veronica to recall each and every place she had lived while married to Willard. Each place would bring stories of violence and abuse as well as horrific things that the two of them had been involved with over the years. The jury would be exposed to unimaginable sinfulness during Veronica's testimony. Everything from physical, mental, and sexual abuse to group sex, and even bestiality would be unveiled during her testimony. To watch her testimony was very sad. Sad that she had allowed herself to get caught up in this lifestyle, and that she appeared to even enjoy certain aspects of the lifestyle. As I watched the tape, I came to realize that much of what I had gone through as a child was of my mother's own doing. Yes, Willard was a mean and hateful man, but as a mother, Veronica had a responsibility to protect and love her children. A responsibility she took lightly and failed to achieve. Veronica chose this lifestyle, and with her choices, she dragged her children and mother through the same turbulent lifestyle that she had chosen. After the defense team completed the initial examination of Veronica Simms, the prosecution took their turn at cross-examination.

The lead prosecutor wasted no time getting to the details surrounding the shooting. The first question he asked was, "How many times that weekend did you ask Mary if she would kill Willard?" Veronica replied,

"I didn't ask Mary to kill him." "That's not what Mary testified to a few days ago, are you saying she's lying?" the prosecutor said. "I'm not going to say Mary lied about it, but I don't remember asking her to shoot him," she replied. "Mrs. Simms, how long had you been planning to kill your husband?" the attorney asked. "I never planned to kill him but I thought about it several times," she exclaimed!. The lead prosecutor's aggressive questioning put Veronica on edge. Her demeanor changed drastically during the cross-examination as she went from meek and subdued to very defensive and sharp. The questions were direct and to the point. As I watched the footage I knew that it had to be difficult for Veronica to answer the questions. At times, I was embarrassed for her. While she would never admit to encouraging me to shoot her husband, the evidence would tell the story Veronica couldn't bear to tell. While questioning Veronica about the inconsistencies in the initial statements she had given to investigators and police officers, the lead prosecutor commented that she had changed her story to "save your bacon didn't you Mrs. Simms!" Her defense team quickly objected to the comment and Judge Coolie stated, "what's your objection?" The defense lawyer stated "your honor this is a very serious matter; 'save your bacon.'" The judge agreed and ordered the prosecutor to rephrase the question, which he did. Even under great pressure and stress of the trial, this comment even made Veronica smirk just a bit. While this would prove to be a lighter moment in the trial, there would be many more serious moments to come. The prosecution spent several more hours questioning Veronica Simms about sexual affairs she had allegedly engaged in, the sexual explicit letters she had written and exchanged with the couple in Chicago, and other demoralizing aspects of her life that painted her as a promiscuous wife and irresponsible mother to her four young children.

While the defense team did a good job of revealing the abusive side of Willard Simms, the prosecution brought forth a lot of damning evidence against Veronica during the trial's rebuttal phase. They showed the jury letters that Veronica had written to family members requesting poison to put in Willard's coffee and other letters describing how she had failed to use enough poison to do the job. One piece of evidence I found extremely disturbing was a letter she had written to my grandmother from her jail prior to being released on bond. The document somehow made its way into the prosecution's hands before the trial and was read aloud to everyone in the courtroom during the trial. The letter read as follows:

Dear Mom,

*I hate this place. Mom, please help me, okay?
Mom, if y'all get to see Mary again, by herself,
make sure there ain't no welfare people listening
and ask her if she could do me a favor. Please, mom,
this is important. My lawyer told me it's up to
Mary— what she says to them. If Mary tells them
I put her up to shoot Willard, then I'm as good as
gone. Do you understand this? I didn't put her up
to do nothing, okay? Ask Mary if she told anybody
that I put her up to shoot Willard, okay? Tell Mary
to tell them that I didn't in no way ask her to shoot
Willard.*

*Please, mom, if she does, I'm gone. If she has,
ask her to tell them it was wrong, please.*

*She ain't the one who's going to prison. It will
be me. God, mom, please talk to her for me, okay?
I'm scared.*

*Mom, I love you. Don't give up on trying to get
me out of jail.*

Veronica

After I heard the prosecuting attorney read the
letter, I realized just how selfish Veronica was and how

she had exploited me, her eleven-year-old daughter, to save herself from going to prison. She wanted me to take full responsibility for killing Willard so that she could walk away unpunished. I didn't speak to either my Veronica or my grandmother prior to the trial, and I told the truth about the shooting regardless of the trial's outcome. While the letter damaged Veronica's chances of exoneration, further testimony showed that she had wanted Willard dead well before 1987.

The prosecution had secured testimony from a man whom Veronica had asked to kill Willard three years prior to 1987. Gary Saxton testified that Veronica had asked him to murder Willard in 1984. As a reward for killing Willard, she allegedly told Saxton that she would marry him if he committed the crime. Saxton also told jurors that he had numerous sexual encounters with Veronica when Willard was working in the oil fields in 1984. Further testimony disclosed that Veronica had asked her son Sammy and her own mother to shoot Willard prior to 1987. In addition to demonstrating her desire to have Willard killed, the prosecution showed that Veronica was a promiscuous wife who had many sexual affairs while married to him. Detailing its case further, the prosecution called to the stand John Bowman and Dean Williams, who confirmed that they both had sexual relations with Veronica. They also attested that

Veronica and Willard had sexual relations with another couple in Glenville on two occasions, bringing up as well the relationship with the couple they had met through the magazine ad. The prosecution went on to introduce many of the explicit letters that Veronica had saved from their days in Glenville, but the investigation never recovered the scrapbook of nude pictures, which probably was burned when Veronica and Willard were separated in 1986. With all this mounting testimony against Veronica, the defense relied heavily on the battered woman syndrome in its case.

One of the key defense witnesses was a Doctor of Physiology who testified that Veronica suffered from battered woman syndrome and that homicide was often the ultimate outcome of this type of abuse. This proved to be the defense's final position—namely, that Willard's abuse of Veronica had prompted the shooting and that homicide was justified to end the abuse once and for all. The prosecution did a good job of refuting this notion by calling its own psychological expert witness to the stand. Dr. William Freemont, a board certified forensic psychologist and professor at the University of West Virginia had been asked to conduct mental assessments of Veronica prior to the trial in an attempt to rule out mental illness or depression as a defense. Veronica met with Dr. Freemont twice at Weston State Hospital for interviews and psychological testing, which proved to be pivotal in the case against her. Dr. Freemont had conducted the Minnesota Multiphase Personality Inventory Test, otherwise known as MMPI, during their first meeting. The test developed a criteria group or profile that fit Veronica's thought process at the time of the shooting. This was a five hundred and fifty-six question test that ruled out psychosis or depression and opened the door for premeditation in the killing of Willard Simms. According to Dr. Freemont, the test showed that Veronica was often "insensitive to others" and "mistrustful in many ways". The second of two tests was slanted more toward Veronica's likelihood to be an abusive parent. This test was known as the Child Abuse Potential Inventory.

The protocol revealed astonishing results relating to Veronica's ability to be a balanced parent and her lack of ability to control conflict within the home. It showed a very low tolerance for children's misbehavior, an inability to cope with stress, a loss of control under the influence of anger, and a high conflict potential given her personality. Dr. Freemont testified that he had administered the Child Abuse Potential Inventory to fifty different women over a twenty four month period and that Veronica's scores were well above the cutoff of two hundred and twenty. The test's scale was zero to four hundred and eighty-six, with a score of one hundred or less representing normal parenting tolerance toward children, and a score of two hundred and twenty or higher signifying a high risk for child abuse. Veronica scored three hundred and sixty-nine, the second highest calibration recorded in Dr. Freemont's administration of the instrument. The test verified that Veronica had a high probability to act out physically when placed under high stress conditions. The information posed a big problem for her defense team, but testimony concerning the two verbal interviews brought even more difficulties for the defense. Dr. Freemont told the jurors that, according to his interviews with her, Veronica confessed to earlier plans to have Willard killed. She had told him about the rat poison and acknowledged that she had had thoughts of killing Willard prior to 1987. Dr. Freemont testified that "Veronica had a strong fear of losing custody of the children and would do whatever she had to do to keep her kids." She reportedly had said, "If he tries to take my kids, I will shoot him in the back of the head." The doctor also read a statement Veronica had made to her mother prior to the shooting: "I will kill him once and for all, sooner or later." Dr. Freemont ended his testimony with sobering words that would etch themselves into each juror's mind. "She showed no remorse that Willard was dead; she was just sorry that she had not done it herself," he said in closing. The question of innocence or guilt was now in the jurors' hands.

After five days of testimony from doctors, lawyers, medical examiners, family, and friends of both Veronica and Willard, the trial concluded. After three hours of deliberation, the jurors signaled to the bailiff that they had reached a decision and were prepared to turn over their decision to Judge Coolie. At 4:20 p.m. on June 23, 1988, the jurors reentered the court room and took their place in the jury box. I was not aware of the verdict, nor was I in the court room to hear it read. Before the verdict was announced, the judge warned everyone in the court room that no response or outburst would be tolerated when the verdict was read. The court reporter then recited the verdict: "We, the people of the jury, find the defendant, Veronica Jean Simms, guilty of murder in the first-degree with mercy to be considered during sentencing."

The verdict echoed throughout the court room and larger community. Veronica Simms was going to prison for a minimum of ten years for the murder of her husband. Upon pronouncement of the verdict, Judge Coolie ordered the bailiffs to remove the prisoner and everyone filed out. A few minutes later Ms. Janie told me that someone wanted to see me. To my surprise, it was Brother Jim. I jumped on his lap and threw my arms around his neck, immediately asking whether I could go home with him. He said, "No, darling, you can't." He tried to explain why, but my young mind couldn't grasp the reason. He said that for my safety I had to live somewhere else farther away. Brother Jim then gave me a letter from Mrs. Kay written on mint green paper with two little heart stickers, one on the outside and another on the inside. When I got back to the Ridgeway's that evening, I went to my room and read the letter:

Dear Mary,

I hope that Brother Jim doesn't forget to give you this. I miss you, Mary. You were always the first one to say I learned my memory verses. I am praying for you, Mary, I know that God is watching over you. Don't forget all those times I told you in class that we have a friend who never leaves us. Lean on your faith, Mary. The whole church is praying for you. Don't forget ever that we love you and that we are here for you. Now give me one of those shy little smiles so that I can feel it where I am.

P.S. Every time I pick up my keys my thoughts are with you because you gave me the key ring. Remember what it said: "A true friend is one who takes you in when the rest of the world has cast you out." It also has a little kitten on it. Thanks again, Mary, for the key ring. It means more to me than anything else.

I love you.
Mrs. Kay

My heart broke into a million pieces over how someone could love me the way they did and not be able to share their lives with me. I didn't realize it at the time, but I would never see them again. I would be at least twenty-two years of age when Veronica became eligible for parole, and my coming years in the foster care system would leave me with more emotional scars and memories for the rest of my life.

The trial behind me, I soon came to the realization that I too was faced with my own sentence of sorts. My sentence was a future in the foster care system and a lifetime bereft of family. There would be no returning to Adrian, no relationships with my halfsiblings, and no more hugs from my grandmother or Brother Jim. Everything I once knew was gone forever. Odd as this might sound, I again found myself longing for family. At the time it seemed as though a dysfunctional family was better than none at all. Everyone I once knew moved forward to start a new chapter in their lives, including myself.

CHAPTER 10

A New Beginning

With the trial now concluded, my cherished grandmother moved back to Cyclone to live with her son. She would live there for several years before passing away in 1991. I never saw her again after the shooting and would be informed of her death well after her burial. Veronica began serving her prison sentence on June 23, 1988. Initially incarcerated for three months at Alderson State Penitentiary, she was transferred to Prunytown Correctional Facility where she served six years before being moved to the Anthony Center in White Sulphur Springs. I visited her in prison a few times over the next ten years.

My halfsiblings were all adopted by the family they had been placed with after the shooting. Brother Jim and his wife Kay continued in the ministry and eventually relocated to Erie, Pennsylvania. There would never be another male figure in my life that I loved as much as Brother Jim. He was the one special person who touched my life the most during those difficult early years. I had been staying with the Ridgeway's for about a month prior to the start of the trial but now it appeared as though I would be living here until I turned eighteen. Everything that had led up to this moment was over. I wanted to forget everything that had happened to me and be a normal kid but the realization that I would forever be in the foster care system was surreal. I knew right away I was different than most kids; I wanted to do everything for myself. No one had ever given me anything, and I certainly didn't think it would start now. I began delivering newspapers in the community so I would have my own money. I went door to door asking neighbors if they would like to start receiving the Weston Democrat, either on a daily basis or weekends. I was quite successful at building my paper route and soon bought a bicycle to reduce my time spent delivering papers. I started eighth grade that year, and begin my own journey into the world of sports. I signed up for basketball and loved it. I enjoyed the team approach, and the relationships it started to give me. Having teammates was like having a family of sorts, you relied on each team member during every aspect of the game, and I was starting to build confidence in myself, and lasting relationships with my teammates.

The Ridgeway's were very busy; they had at times an upwards of thirteen foster children living in the home. Surprisingly though everything seemed to run quite smoothly. I was the only one who was playing sports at the time and I had to stay after school almost every day for practice. Practice lasted from half past three to half past five. So afterward, I would have to catch a ride back to the Ridgeway's house. I would often walk home from practice to keep from being a burden on my foster parents. I hated feeling like I was a burden, so I would do whatever I could to limit the amount of inconvenience I caused the people in my life. I had built up a very tough exterior persona, but on the inside of me, I was filled with emptiness and pain. Every day it seemed I longed for a family to love me, to really want me. I wanted to be a joyful addition to someone's life, not a burden. I remember on several occasions the Ridgeway's adopting other children, and wondered why no one wanted to adopt me. I would often think of my brothers and sister, and I was happy they found a home, where they were the only children. Their adopted family had their own biological children, who were already grown. They embraced the children and accepted them lovingly as their own siblings.

I worked hard in sports and I always wanted the Ridgeway's to come to my games and cheer for me but it would never happen. They could never seem to make it to any of my games but this would not deter me from being the best athlete I could be. I lived with the Ridge way's for about five years altogether. Though I had many good times, I had some bad as well. At one point, Mrs. Ridgeway had taken in a foster child named Ricardo. Ricardo was about sixteen years old at the time and was a bit of a wild child.

He smoked marijuana and was very disobedient. There was even a rumor that he was growing marijuana in the woods behind the Ridgeway's house. I had become heavily involved in sports and I found it to be a great outlet for me. Many evenings, even after practice, I would run on a trail behind our house. Mrs. Ridgeway became suspicious and accused me of getting involved with marijuana or something of the sort. I'm not sure how she came to this determination, but it would bring unwanted changes. As a result of her unfounded suspicions, I was forbidden to leave the yard. She told me the restriction was because I was a foster child and that all foster children had to stay in the yard. This really angered me. I had always tried to be the very best kid I could be. I played every sport that I could, I took a job delivering papers, I helped out with housework, and I even helped with outdoor chores such as mowing, painting, and gardening. I knew that

I had been given a second chance and even though they were not my parents, I still felt a responsibility to show my appreciation the only way I knew how. Yet this did not stop her from forbidding me to leave the yard. The basketball goal was located outside the fenced area, and she forbade me from simply playing basketball. I was very angry and could not understand how she could do this to me. I didn't even know what marijuana looked like and certainly had no desire to get involved with it. Mrs. Ridgeway admitted that she knew I wasn't doing drugs, but she insisted that she had to protect me. I had grown increasingly angry over the situation and had begun to lash out; I told her many times that I hated her for what she was doing to me. I knew that the unfounded broken trust meant that I must find a way to move on. Once I was fifteen and knew everything there was to know about life, or so I thought, I met a young woman that lived a few houses down from the Ridgeway family. I saw her when I delivered her newspaper on the weekends. She was a parole officer for the state of West Virginia and had no children of her own, just her and her husband. She would often say to me, "I wish we could adopt you." I would simply smile. I never allowed myself to fully imagine that someone could really want me to be their child. I was a throwaway kid and I knew it. Nobody really wanted me,

I was just a kid in the system, and it was someone's job to take care of me until I was eighteen years old.

I told that the Ridgeway family had confined me to the yard without reason and she said she might be able to help. She told me she knew a lady who was a teacher at the high school I attended. She taught special education children. She told me that she had only had one other foster child, but that she did not have any at the time. I listened to her intently with one thought in mind–leaving the Ridgeway's. I knew I had to go and I would jump at any opportunity to make it happen. All the years I spent with the Ridgeway family and now I can't even leave the yard. I refused to be imprisoned, and as I watched their "real" kids go play with neighboring children, ride their bikes, and play basketball I knew I had to go. I just wanted to be a "real" kid myself; I wanted and needed someone to refer to me as their daughter for once, not as their "foster child". I hated hearing those words, even to this day those words echo through me and I cringe at the thought of ever hearing them again. As I look back, I realize that I was one of the first foster children she had that was becoming a teenager while living with the Ridgeway family. I believe that Mrs. Ridgeway had the mentality that all foster kids were troubled kids–which they are. Most of them have had their lives completely turned upside down. Most

Foster Children have a difficult time trusting people. They feel as though they have no stability in their lives; forgotten and lost in the system that was designed to protect them. I knew that the Ridgeway family could never provide me with the family life I was in need of, and with the heavy restrictions placed upon me, I had to move on.

After a few weeks had passed, I was told that a special education teacher, Mrs. Johnson, was interested in taking me in. Mrs. Johnson had called me to set up a time to meet with her and her husband. We all went out to dinner together and had a long conversation. I told them what had happened at the Ridgeway's and that I really wanted to be in a place where I felt like I had a family. As we discussed my past, Mrs. Johnson began to sob and I too became overwhelmed with emotions. I felt as though someone understood me at last. Another couple weeks had passed, Mrs. Ridgeway and I were constantly arguing. I had already packed up my belongings in anticipation of moving to the Johnson's home. After packing feverishly for several days, I came home from basketball practice and discovered that everything had been unpacked. I ask Mrs. Ridgeway why she did this and she said that she didn't want me to leave. Needless to say, at this point, my decision had been made.

A couple of days later, I had confirmation that the following Saturday that the Johnson's would be picking me up to come and live with them. I was so excited. I would be the only kid at the Johnson's and I began to dream about having a real family. As the week passed, I couldn't control the growing excitement I felt inside. That Saturday came and they were supposed to be there to pick me up at ten o'clock in the morning. As I awaited their arrival with great excitement, I soon realized that the hour of ten o'clock in the morning had come and gone. I called their home and no answer, so I thought perhaps they were on there a way to get me. Hours passed, and still no word from the Johnson family. I felt a sick feeling in my stomach. Had the family I dreamed of having changed their mind? I had dealt with so many disappointments in my life, could this be just another one? A short while later, the phone rang at the Ridgeway's; it was Mrs. Johnson. I was real nervous to talk to her. Were they calling to tell me they had changed their mind? I reluctantly put the receiver up to my ear and said hello. Mrs. Johnson said, "Hello Mary we haven't forgotten about you, we will pick you around four o'clock in the afternoon." I obliged and then told her that there was a homecoming dance that evening at the high school and that I had been planning to go to the dance for some time. She said that would be fine and extended an explanation as to why they were late picking me up. She told me that her mother and father had come in from Parkersburg to visit. I already began to feel a sense of not belonging. Nonetheless, Mr. and Mrs. Johnson showed up as they said they would around four to pick me up. I eagerly packed all my stuff into their truck and was off to start a new life. I was extremely nervous and somewhat shy. The reality of moving into someone else's home that I really did not know and had not even visited started to creep into my head.

When I arrived at my new destination, I was only able to unpack my clothes and personal belongings; I needed to start getting ready for the homecoming dance. I realized rather quickly, that I didn't have anything to wear. Mrs. Johnson said she thought maybe she might have something I could wear, so we scouted through her closet, and came up with a nice ash gray skirt suit. I thanked her very much, and before long I was off to the dance. My homecoming date was only fifteen years old and he did not have a driver's license at the time, so we planned to meet at the dance at seven o'clock in the evening. Mrs. Johnson was kind enough to drive me to the school that evening and ask me when I would like to be picked up. I told her the dance ended at ten o'clock in the evening, and she assured me she would see me shortly after that. I had a nice evening and when the dance was over my boyfriend's dad came to pick him up. I was confident that Mrs. Johnson would soon be arriving to pick me up, but ten o'clock came and went, as it had earlier that day when I waiting for them to pick me up at the Ridgeway's. My boyfriend and his dad insisted on waiting with me until someone came. Half past ten came, then eleven o'clock I began to get nervous. I didn't even have a quarter to call them to see if something had happened. My boyfriend's dad offered to drive me home and I reminded him that I had just moved in with the Johnson family earlier that evening, and I wasn't really sure how to get to their house. So he offered me some change, drove me to the pantry store a block away from the school, and I called Mrs. Johnson from a payphone.

She answered, "Hello." I said, "Hi, this is Mary, I was wondering if maybe you were coming to pick me up?" She said, "Oh my God Mary I am so sorry, I fell asleep on the couch, and I totally forgot about you." What a stinger to my heart–"forgot about you." Well, I thought, I have only been there a few short hours and she is really not use to having a minor child around. So I reasoned to myself why I was forgotten, I offered to start walking and meet her so she would not have to drive so far. The Johnson's home was about fifteen miles from the school. I was used to walking anyway; I did it many times when I lived with the Ridgeway's. I was already starting to feel like a burden. I would have much rather walked back to the Johnson's home than to call and ask if someone was coming to pick me up. I had an enormous amount of pride and I could hardly bring myself to ask anything from anybody. When Mrs. Johnson arrived she was apologetic for falling asleep. I assured her there was no need to be sorry, I understood.

The next day, Mr. Johnson helped me put my waterbed together, something I had bought for myself during the time I was delivering newspapers, and I begin to decorate my room, and try to give myself a sense of belonging. It was tough, living with new people. They were so young, early thirties, and as time passed I begin to realize, they were more like an older brother and sister rather than parents. In fact Mr. Johnson's parents had adopted a little girl when she was a baby, and she was now fifteen as well. So, in actuality, he did have a sister who was my age.

I continued my love for sports, and band throughout high school. The Johnson's did not get involved much in my extracurricular activities. In fact they really didn't get involved at all. I never fully developed a close relationship with the Johnson's as I had hoped I would. I called them only by their first names as well, never Mom or Dad, this too was just not meant to be. As always, I would begin to think back to Jim and Kay McCall, I never forgot them. I wondered many times, if they knew where I was, what I was doing. Did they even care at this point? Of course they did, I told myself, they cared for me, and I felt their special love inside my heart. It would not go away that easily, it didn't for me. Though I faced many disappointments relating to family and acceptance, I plunged myself deep into sports. It was my life and I loved it. I did alright academically, but I was no scholar. I focused much of my attention and energy into team sports and I knew I had a future in athletics. Unfortunately, the Johnson family felt quite differently about this.

College Life

Throughout the next few years, I became one of the best athletes at Lewis County High School. I topped the volleyball club in service points with a record of two hundred and twenty-five points my senior year. I was also one of only two athletes to advance to the West Virginia State Track Meet. Ironically, the meet fell on the day I was graduating from high school on May 29, 1993. But I was there and finished ninth in shotput and eleventh in the discus throw. Not my best, but I was competing with the state's very best athletes, so I was happy overall. Besides that, I was graduating from high school that evening. It was an accomplishment that I was very proud of. I was voted Most Athletic by my peers, and coaches. I received First Team All North Central Athletic Conference Honors in Softball, Volleyball, and Track. I also earned the Minutemen Athletic Club Scholarship, but my proudest moment was getting inducted into the Athletic Hall of Fame. I was only the fourth female athlete to achieve this honor since the annual award began in 1977. I am proud of who I became as a young adult. I experienced one of the most horrific childhoods imaginable, but not the worst. As I always say, "no matter how bad you think you have it, someone, somewhere always has it worse." I didn't want or expect pity from anyone; instead, I needed encouragement. I wanted to overcome this horrendous stigma that I feared could be attached to me forever. I wanted people to know the real Mary Elizabeth Bailey.

The real person inside of me was not a murderer; she was a loving and caring young girl who longed for the love and affection of a family. I needed the acceptance of my peers, in order to continue building my self-confidence. I needed support from my teachers. These individuals didn't know about me, and about what happened to me as an eleven year old girl, and that's the way I wanted it. I wanted to be treated like everyone else–normal. I did a great job hiding the pain of not having a family. So much of the life I built has been to make someone proud. The problem I found was that no one who cared enough to be proud of me. Of all my years throughout school sports, parent's night was always the worst for me. All my teammates had their parents there when their names were called, but for me, I walked alone. While it hurt me deeply, most people never knew the pain I felt and the few who did never said a word.

I went through my teen years as a foster child never adopted or loved the way I needed to be loved. Soon after high school, I was dropped off in Huntington, West Virginia by my foster family, and started my life as an adult. As a seventeen-year-old freshman at Marshall University, I was isolated from everyone and everything I once knew, starting over once again. I remember the day Mr. Johnson and his brother Greg dropped me off. It was two weeks before school started and no one was on campus as of yet. Mr. & Mrs. Johnson were a bit upset at me because I had chosen to go to Marshall University instead of Glenville State College. So they told me that they would drop me off when they could, but made it clear they were not going to make a special trip. Mr. Johnson was a general contractor, he owned his own business and had bid on a job that just so happened to be in the vicinity of Huntington. I called the university in advance of my early arrival to ensure I could stay at the dorms. Mrs. Johnson said I needed to find a place to stay in Huntington or find someone else to take me. Fortunately for me, I was allowed to stay on campus for free until class started. My first days there, I was like a little kid. I wanted to go everywhere and see everything. I remember the first thing on campus that beckoned my attention was the fountain. "The Crash" of November 14, 1970, of Marshall University's football team. I stood there in awe of the memory of each person that lost their life that rainy night. It was there I learned the reason behind the chant "We Are… Marshall." I enjoyed campus life a great deal. I was only seventeen, so I couldn't go out to the clubs, with any of the new friends I was meeting. It was August, and I didn't turn eighteen until October. Nonetheless, I didn't mind. I became involved in sports; after all, I had earned an athletic scholarship and planned to make the most of it. I discovered a new sport during my time at Marshall…Rugby. I was tossing a football one afternoon with a friend of mine, and a girl from the Rugby team asked me if I may be interested in playing. She told me tryouts were within a week, and that I looked like I would be a really good fit. I thought why not and the rest is history. I loved it. Our team went 150 that year. It was a very aggressive sport, but I was a true tomboy and for me, it was very therapeutic to vent the frustrations that were deep inside of me from my childhood.

The semester went by rather quickly, and it was Christmas break before I knew it. I had kept in touch weekly with the Johnson family and let them know how things were going and what I was doing. I told them that school would be out for a couple of weeks for the break, and ask when they might be able to come to pick me up. Mrs. Johnson replied, "You will need to find your own way back if you want to come back here." While I was not totally surprised by her reply, I found myself in a state of shock because I had no idea how on earth I would get back to Weston. I knew couldn't stay at Marshall during the break, everything would be closed, and there would be no one on campus. I expressed my concern to my roommate, and she offered me a ride. She lived in Parkersburg, West Virginia and going to Weston was well out of her way, but her and her mother graciously drove me back to the Johnson's house.

This treatment continued over the next couple of semesters. I felt like such a burden on everyone. I soon came to realize that I had no home to return to. It was just a house in Weston where I no longer felt welcome. I was now eighteen years old and when you're a foster kid, eighteen means you are on your own. My time at Marshall left me feeling as though I was a failure. Without the guidance and support of parents, I was unable to fulfill my dream of a college degree. After forgoing my education, I got a medial job and moved into an off campus apartment. My adult life had just begun, and I knew that I faced an uphill battle.

CHAPTER 12

Parole Hearing

Poor choices and alcohol abuse were beginning to creep into my young life, and I knew that I had to turn things around before I ended up just like my mother. Once again I turned to God and put faith in him to help me overcome all that I was facing as a young adult. Shortly thereafter, I got involved with an organization known as the Jehovah's Witnesses and found peace in weekly bible study. I spent much of my time attending fellowship meetings and forging relationships with other Christians. This religion seemed to really fit into my lifestyle. Jehovah's Witnesses did not celebrate birthdays or holidays, and that was fine by me. After all, I didn't even have a family to celebrate those occasions with anyway.

A few weeks before leaving for a Christian convention in Columbus, Ohio, I received a phone call from a young woman who claimed to be my sister. I was taken back a bit by this revelation for obvious reasons. The only sister I actually knew was Sara, yet this per son claimed to be the daughter of my biological father Tim Boyd. Out of curiosity, I pursued the conversation. After all, part of me was curious about what my father looked like especially since I was the only one in my family with red hair. The caller informed me that my biological father wanted to meet me because he had always been curious about the person I had become. Somehow, Tim had learned that Veronica had used me to murder her husband. When she asked whether I wanted to talk to him, I agreed, and we made arrangements to meet. I met my biological father for the first and last time in Shady Springs, Ohio. At the time I was twenty-one years old. The meeting brought little comfort and left me with a familiar feeling, that of being without a family.

There was no bond and relationship to build on. Tim Boyd died of lung cancer a few months after our meeting. I never cried a tear, nor did I attend his funeral. He wasn't my father. My father was a memory of Brother Jim, the man whose heart was as big as the sky. While I had no father figure in my life, Veronica was now keeping in close contact with me for her own selfish reasons. A short while after my biological father passed away, she sent me a letter stating that she would be up for parole, and ask if I would come and speak on her behalf. Ten years had passed quickly, it was now 1998.

As a supportive daughter, I went before the parole board and pleaded for her release, though I spoke with an empty heart and painful memories. Still, the words seemed to roll smoothly from my tongue and touch even the coldest of hearts that day. As some fought back their tears, I began to realize that they too could feel my pain, the broken spirit of twenty-three-year-old women. Some things never change. After only thirty minutes of another familiar moment of deliberation, Veronica's fate hung in the hands of a new group of men and women. As I awaited the decision, I wondered what things might be like if she were released. Would Veronica want to be the mother she never was to me? And what about the other children? Would she want to have a relationship with them? More importantly, would they want to have a relationship with her?

"Mary, they're ready for us." These were the words of Carolyn Hobbs, who had come to support Veronica. She was the same lady who had testified ten years earlier on my mother's behalf regarding battered woman's syndrome. Before long, I found myself back in the room where moments earlier I had poured out my heart for a mother I never knew, whose love I had yet to experience. We all sat in silence awaiting the parole board's decision. "Veronica Simms, the parole board hereby approves your release." It was a moment of relief, but still there was more to be said. Veronica had to make sure she went to her probation meetings every week, and she had to pass drug and alcohol testing. She again was instructed not to go to Upshur County where she had been banned for life by Judge Coolie. Before long I found myself in a caretaker role for my own mother, and yet again she would bring more disappointment into my life. Why, I now ask myself, did I think she could be the mother I never had? Even after her incarceration, Veronica still lived just as irresponsibly as she had when I was a little girl. Once again, though she never changed, I took to the battleground and fought for the enemy, and I helped her find a job and a place of her own.

During the next year, I drove her to and from probation meetings. When she began talking about wanting a baby, I was incredulous. Veronica could barely care for herself. How on earth, given her history as a mother, could she possibly think she could care for another person? Recalling the brutal life I lived when I was younger, I couldn't imagine what was going through her mind. After she fulfilled her probation obligations, she was officially a free woman, with no one to answer to anymore. Although I urged her not to have another child, Veronica became pregnant at the age of thirty-nine. She carried the baby for a full five months until fetal mortality forced her into premature delivery of a stillborn baby boy. After this act of selfishness, I knew that if I were going to make it in this world, I had to get as far away from my Veronica as I could. Had I known the details of the case at the time of the parole hearing, I would have had a hard time pleading for Veronica's freedom.

CHAPTER 13

Final Move

In 1999, I moved to Charlotte, North Carolina and never looked back. I started a new job and went back to school to earn my nursing degree. Life in Charlotte was a fresh start for me with more uncharted water, but I embraced it. I lay to rest the memories of my past and began to build a life that I could be proud of. When I started thinking of my grandmother and Brother Jim, both of whom I missed greatly, it occurred to me that I could see them again. All I had to do was to open Pandora's Box (the videos of the 1988 trial footage). I was thirty-two years old before I decided to view the videos of the trial, never having looked at them since receiving them when I was sixteen. Perhaps I simply had not wanted to know the truth about the situation. Later, however, the reality of the woman I had become, and the past I seemed to have forgotten made me wonder what might be hiding on each of those videos. I was scared. I knew there would be information on the videos that would shock me. Sometimes it easier to believe what you have come to know, rather than what you don't know. I was unsure but I knew that in order to start the healing process, I needed to know the truth.

After viewing the videos, I realized why for so long I had avoided watching the trial footage. It reinforced the ugly truth about the kind of selfish and manipulative woman Veronica was, someone who had brought my grandmother back into her life not only to get her money but also to use me as a pawn in killing her abusive husband. After all, she knew how much I disliked him and how he felt toward me. Her futile attempts in getting anyone else to kill Willard went unfulfilled. The more I watched the trial footage, the more enraged I became with Veronica. I was essentially nothing more to her than a get out of jail free card, or so she thought. I also realized how her behavior had fueled Willard's anger and how poor a mother she had been to all four of her children. My relationship with Veronica now involves nothing more than an occasional phone call, usually initiated by her. Sometimes many months go by without a word being exchanged. Unfortunately for her, she stills bathes in the sorrow and pity that has long been a distant memory. A past that will most likely haunt her for the rest of her life. The realization of growing old without the love and companionship of her children...that's the haunting part. She looks endlessly for someone to feel sorry for her, to tell her that she deserves better, to reassure her that her children should be ashamed of themselves for not reaching out, and helping her. She lives inside a bubble of self-pity. Spending time in prison is not an acceptance of responsibility, it's a sentence put forth by the court system for the poor choices that were made as a parent. I have not seen Veronica in person since I left Huntington in 1999, and I deliberately refer to her only by her given name. To be referred to as "mother" is an earned honor and privilege, not an automatic right.

CHAPTER 14

Closing Doors

I have worked diligently to find Brother Jim and Kay, knowing that my life would not be complete until I did. My journey to have them in my life again had once again taken me down an emotional path, but it has been worth every moment. There were times I would wonder if tragedy had taken them from me, but I quickly dismissed this incredulous thought as a mere deterrent in halting my progress. Losing them before I ever found them would have been too overwhelming for me to accept. Though they have been absent from my life for more than twenty years, they were still very much present in my heart. After many phone calls and internet searches, my determination to find them would be rewarded on April 27, 2009. This would be one of the happiest days of my life.

That feeling became reality when I nervously but eagerly dialed the numbers, that I hoped this time would find a familiar voice on the other end of the line. "Hello," the voice on the other end shyly said. I knew the voice like it was my own. "Hi is this Kay?" I said with my heart about to explode with joy. "Yes, yes it is, Mary is that you?" she replied. I couldn't believe it; she immediately recognized my voice as well. "Yes, this is Mary!" I exclaimed. My eyes quickly filled with tears of joy. The longing of my heart to hear the familiar voice of my past, the voice that calmed many of my days as a young child. "Oh Mary, Brother Jim is going to be so happy, he has talked about you everywhere we have ever been, he won't believe it." She informed me that he was at work and that he would be home around five o'clock. We talked awhile longer and as we did, much of the hurt, the longing, and the pain of not having them in my life began to lift and a gentle peace landed softly on the edges of my heart. The emotion and the feeling I begin to experience as I traveled back to a place in my past that was always warm, comfortable, and welcoming felt so good. I felt a huge part of my emptiness lift from me at that very moment. I knew this was the love I had been missing since the day I walked out of that courtroom as a brokenhearted little girl in June 1988 after asking Brother Jim if he would take me home with him. I never wanted anything as bad as I did a family and here I was again presented with an opportunity to have just that.

While I eagerly awaited Brother Jim's phone call, I could hardly stand being inside my own skin... five o'clock could not come fast enough. I don't typically wish my days away, but after twenty-two years of not having him in my life, the minutes now awaiting his phone call was nothing more than an obstacle in my path. At two minutes past five o'clock my phone rings and my heart pounds with excitement. I am so nervous yet so eager to talk to the man who I genuinely felt was the father I never had. I took a deep breath as I picked up my phone. "Hello," I said. "Mary is that you?" he replied. "Yes," I replied. "Little Mary—Mary, Mary quit contrary I can't believe it!" With a smile I said, "Yes sir its little Mary." As we talked and attempted to catch up on twenty years of living apart, I began to hear his voice crack ever so slightly as the emotion overtook both of us. He said that he has told everyone he meets about me. He told me that he had thought of me endlessly over the years and often wondered about where I was living, what I was doing.

"You know I wanted to adopt you when you were a little girl?" Brother Jim said. "Yes," I replied. "Judge Coolie said we couldn't adopt you because of the close proximity to where we lived and where everything happened, he said it was for your safety, and that you needed to be moved far away from Upshur County," he explained.

"Yes I know, I hated that, I wanted to be with you and Mrs. Kay so bad," I said. "I know dear, Kay and I cried for days afterward, wondering if we would ever see you again." Jim went on to tell me that he was pastoring a church in Ridgeville, South Carolina, and of course he had told his congregation all about me as well. He asked me if I would come and share my story with the congregation at his church. I was a bit apprehensive, to say the least. I had never talked openly about the tragedies of that fateful winter night in 1987, but I felt a sense of calm when Jim told me he would be right beside me as I told the story of my past. I knew deep within that this might be an opportunity to share with people who needed to hear that there is power in believing, power in healing, and power in love. We set a date to meet on May 15, 2009. I would plan to travel to his hometown of Moncks Corner, South Carolina. We talked awhile longer and finally we had to say goodbye. Hanging up with the phone after the conversation ended brought back a flood of emotions. I sat there in silence, stunned. It had taken me months to find him and in an instance he is gone again. I found myself wanting to call him back almost immediately, but I knew we would talk again very soon.

A few weeks later on May 15, 2009, I set out on this journey, my heart swelled with excitement. I was going to see the man who I had not seen in over twenty years. This was really a dream come true for me. I arrived safely at the hotel, heart racing with excitement, I was able to get checked in, and attempt to calm myself down with a warm shower. As the anticipation of seeing Brother Jim continued to grow, the more nervous I became. What would he think of me? Would he even recognize me? His last memory of me was that of a little girl, I'm a thirty-one-year-old woman now. As my mind raced with questions, the phone in my hotel room rang. I thought it's him, he's here, and the moment has arrived at last to see the man that meant so much to me as a child. I answered the phone knowing he was only a few steps from my room and we would soon be standing face to face once again. "Mary? Hey honey, it's me, I'm upfront." He said in a joyful tone. "Okay. I'll be right there," I replied.

As I gathered my thoughts, I took a look in the mirror as I was about to walk out the door, and down the long corridor. I took a moment to thank God for this day, to thank him for keeping Brother Jim safe all these years, and for keeping me safe as well. I opened the door and began the walk from my present back to my past; a very beautiful and loving part of my past. My heels clicked loudly against the tile floor as I approached the hotel lobby and my head lowered ever so slightly as if to say to my high heeled shoes "be quiet." As I looked up, Jim was standing there at the end of the hall, all six foot seven inches of him. His smile was as radiant as I remembered as a child. His distinct salt and pepper hair was now white as snow. I smiled as big as my face would allow and lifted my arms to embrace him. It was Brother Jim, the man whom I longed to be my Dad. We were both happier than any two people could be. We knew that though life had pulled us apart for whatever reason, it was obvious that time had never taken anything away. It became clear to everyone that evening that we were so happy to have this moment with each other. Over dinner, we spent hours catching up on the last twenty years. He was so proud of me, he just couldn't stop beaming. It humbles me greatly to say that, I knew why he was so proud. I had overcome a great tragedy and had blossomed into someone who the world would never realize had overcome so much adversity. Kay couldn't be with us on this particular weekend, but she as always was in our thoughts and discussions.

We enjoyed our weekend together and on Sunday, May 17, 2009, we drove to his church to share our testimony. I felt a calmness come over me that morning because I knew God was with me and Brother Jim. Up to this point, I had not called Brother Jim "Dad". I felt it, I knew it, but I just couldn't say it. After all, I had never really called anyone Dad before this time. I was now thirty-three-years-old and the thought of having a Dad was as wonderful as I had imagined it would be. However, the reality of having a father figure in my life after all these years did seem a bit weird, but I was grateful and happy to have him in my life once again. We arrived at the church about an hour before the service was to begin. He showed me around, encouraged me to stand at the pulpit, and try to become as comfortable as possible. The reality was quickly setting in, I felt nauseous. I can't do this. I'm not a public speaker. I get nervous when I talk in a public. Everyone at the church, except for Brother Jim, is a stranger to me. My palms were beginning to get sweaty and I felt as if I was about to pass out. It was then that Jim reminded me that all the people were my brothers and sisters through Christ and that they were all here to support us in our testimony. I immediately felt relief and knew that he was right. If this testimony could reach out to just one lost soul, then all my anxiety would not be in vain.

Shortly thereafter, members and visitors began arriving at the church. I began meeting everyone and they begin telling me that they had heard so much about me. Sunday school started at ten o'clock. This would be the first time I had been to Sunday school since I was a little girl. It was a lot of fun, and everyone seemed genuinely nice. They made me feel very comfortable. After Sunday school concluded, I mingled a bit with a few of the members. As always, Brother Jim flashed a smile and a wink my way, and I immediately felt that everything was going to be okay. It was almost time to start the service... eleven o'clock was quickly approaching.

As I sat there on the front row of the church pew, which is where I always sat as a little girl when Brother Jim preached, I found myself thinking about all the times I had sat awaiting his sermon as a small child. I didn't sit on the front row because he was soft spoken. His voice was always engaging, yet loving. I sat on the front row because as a little girl, I felt safe when I was near him. The nearer I could be to him, the safer I would feel. It was then I begin to realize the significance of our journey through life together. I realized so many of the things that happened in my life affected not only me but him as well. For a moment, I felt sad that he had to go through his life wondering what happened to me, wondering if he made a lasting impact on my heart that would lead me to make good choices as an adult. I wondered if he felt guilty for not being able to prevent what happened to me as a little girl. Had the tragic events of February 1987 infiltrated his mind over the past twenty-two years? How could he have known?

He never knew Veronica or Willard. He only knew what I told him, and at the time I only told him that I didn't want to go back home. I only told him that I wanted to stay with him and Kay.

My attention quickly turned back to the present as Brother Jim was about to start the sermon and tell the first part of our story. As he approached the pulpit that morning, I remembered how in awe I was as a child at how tall he was when he stood in front of the congregation. His very presence was as engaging, as it was powerful. As he began to talk, I could tell that emotion was beginning to overtake him, I prayed to keep my composure, I needed to stay focused, and to not let my emotions overtake me. If I didn't take control of my emotions, I knew I would never get through my part of the testimony. I wanted to do this for Brother Jim as well as myself. He said something that I will never forget, "this young lady sitting on the front row is my daughter, and I am her Dad." I was in utter disbelief. Not because it was something we both knew without ever having to say it, but because I had never heard it. I had never been anyone's daughter, and I certainly never expected to hear someone say that they were my Dad. I felt this warm feeling radiate over my entire body. After all the years of praying to find him, that day was finally here. We shared an emotional embrace as he wrapped up his part of the story and I began mine.

I told the congregation of the harrowing life I lived. I shared scriptures from the Bible that comforted me throughout my life. My favorite one is in Psalm 71:58 (NCV), "Lord you are my hope, I have trusted in you since I was young. I have depended on you since I was born; you helped me even on the day of my birth. I will always praise you. I am an example to many people, because you are my strong protection. I am always praising you; all day long I honor you." As I finished my part of the testimony, I shared the letter that Pastor McCall's wife, Kay, had written to me in 1988 when I was just thirteen years old. I talked of the many times I had moved, seventeen to be exact, since I got that letter, and haw I had never let it far from my sight. It brought back the memories of reading that letter the first time Brother Jim had given it to me as a little girl; the pain, the confusion, the heartache. All that is long past, now I can look up and see what I couldn't after reading the letter twenty-two years ago.

As Brother Jim brought the service to an end, he asked me to stand with him during the benediction. A young lady came forward that day and decided to accept Jesus Christ as her Lord and Savior and to join the church. We prayed a loving prayer to our heavenly

Father, really thanked him for this opportunity, and the many wonderful blessings He lovingly bestows on each of us. The congregation lined up one by one to welcome their newest member, and to share their appreciation for what I overcame. Several shared stories of their own trials and tribulations with me, as they were leaving the church that day. It was a glorious time to share with people who were initially complete strangers, but who are now an extension of my spiritual family. I had to leave for home shortly after the service ended. Leaving was more difficult than I had imagined it would be. Brother Jim put his arm around me and walked me to my car. He embraced me and I held on tighter than ever. I didn't want to let go, I was afraid to say goodbye. Though I knew we would always make time for each other. I couldn't help but feel the same pain that I felt the last time we had embraced like this more than twenty-two years ago.

CHAPTER 15

A Life Defined

It's easy to imagine where a person such as myself could end up. Many people in my situation don't choose the road less traveled. Many people choose not to accept responsibility for their actions when it's their very actions that take them down the same road they have previously traveled. Many blame everyone else around them for the choices they make in their own lives. This would not be the case for me. I don't say this because I think I am better than anyone else, but because it's my life and what I choose to make of it. People come from all walks of life. Some are born with silver spoons in their mouth, some with rusty ones, and others with no spoons at all. No matter how you are born into this world, no one escapes life without some form of trial or tribulation. These trials come in many forms and some may be easier to deal with than others. Nonetheless, our trials are what make us stronger. They are just another step in our journey through this amazing thing called life.

It's hard to explain the pain and emptiness of life without the love and stability of a family. I can tell you it's a lonely and empty place to be. Families don't always come in all the same way. For most, families spawn from biological parents having a mom and dad determined to raise their child to the best of their ability. For others, it may be through the love of adoption. Like me, many have the love of their grandparents to keep them strong. While much of my childhood was filled with unimaginable loneliness and despair, much of my sense of fulfillment came through the love and genuine compassion of God... no DNA, no adoption papers. I feel that God put Brother Jim and Kay in my life to give me hope and guidance that would not have been otherwise. I think many times blessings come into our lives and we don't even realize. I believe deep within my heart that God has always looked out for me, holding my hand as I walked alone. He didn't put the tragedy of February 1987 on me, but he was there for me every step of my journey giving me the strength to rise above.

I knew that no matter how many people journeyed in and out of my life, God was constant–always there when I needed to talk, when I needed to cry, when I needed to believe in something more than I believed in at the moment. Knowing that every step of the way he is there holding tight not only to my hand but my heart. All the insecurities I had as a child are no longer things I think about. I found ways to rise above. My past has molded me to be the person I am today. I have learned so much from life and the challenges presented to me along the way. If someone would ask me if I could change anything about my past what would it be? I would tell them... nothing. Not because I am proud of everything that happened along the way, but because I am proud of the woman I am today. Life molded me. The script of negativity that could have been written long ago, for who I would be today, would be shattered through my dedication and determination to succeed in life. I found a way to move beyond my horrific childhood and become a successful and responsible adult.

Through all of this, I have learned to forgive myself, as well as others for what happened. I must forgive in order to be forgiven. My spiritual peace is far too important to live my life with anger and hate in my heart. All things happen for a reason, though I cannot condone the taking of another person's life. I am so glad that I have lived each day with my eyes wide open because otherwise, I would have missed so many wonderful things. No matter what we are going through in life, we must stand tall and face each challenge. Life never promised any of us a rose garden, and, even if it had, roses have thorns and sometimes they prick.

Epilogue

How very true it is that roses no matter how beautiful indeed have thorns. So, careful handling is required... much like life. Ironically, I am writing this epilogue February 18, 2020 thirty-three years to the month since that cold fateful night in 1987. So much has changed over the years. Unfortunately, my brother Sammy and sister Sara could not seem to escape the life we were born into. Jacob Lee didn't get a chance to see what life was about; he passed away in his early twenties from complications related to muscular dystrophy. My biological mother Veronica stills lives in the same city she was paroled to in West Virginia. She has had many struggles and disappointments. She has no relationship with her children, certainly not with me (this is of course by choice). Even worse no relationship with God. I am not better than anyone; I have chosen to make a better life than the one I was born into. That is a choice we all have, an opportunity we must take if we are to break the chains of this terrible cycle many of us find ourselves in. We can feel sorry for ourselves but at the end of the day, where does that get us? Where does it take us? Most importantly, who does it make us?

As for myself, well, I am now forty-four years old. After college life in Huntington, West Virginia, I moved to Charlotte, North Carolina. Met a wonderful man, we married a year later in October of 2000, and have been together for nearly twenty years. We worked together buying foreclosures and did some house flipping. Those were some of the best years. Over time he encouraged me to go back to school to get my nursing license. I did just that and in 2004 I graduated. I have worked in many areas of nursing since then, but my favorite has always been geriatrics. Maybe I see my sweet grandmother and grandfather in each and every life I have had the privilege to care for. In 2012 we opened a uniform store for nurses and healthcare workers. It was something we were both passionate about at the time and now we currently own three stores in North and South Carolina. I won't tell you this has been easy because it has not. What I will tell you it that it has pushed me to the breaking point on many occasions. It has caused marital difficulties that have led to separation and talk of divorce. It has shown me that people who claim to be your friends will shop with your competitor instead of supporting you. It has tested my faith in God and has made me question everything. What may seem to some as a wonderful opportunity to be your own boss to start your own business, they see only what they can see from the outside. What they don't and cannot see is the late nights along with the stress of making payroll, bills, inventory, and the toll it takes on relationships. Relationships that were once so strong, would take a mighty army to tear it down. Life begins to crumble beneath you, you question every decision you ever made, and wonder if it was worth it. You lie awake at three o'clock in the morning heart racing feeling as though you're losing everything and there is nothing you can do to stop the avalanche from collapsing. And all you care about is your marriage, but you have your life savings invested in your business. Pulling yourself up and realizing that you now have a marriage to work on and a business to work on. It becomes a very daunting and seemingly impossible task. Satan wants to see destruction and he throws everything he possibly can at you—everything.

To the ones who may be reading this, stay strong. I know words are easy to say, actions are hard to do. But in that time in my life when everything was going in the wrong direction and I couldn't seem to figure it out, time was passing things were getting worse and worse. I stopped and looked back only to realize the missing link in all of it – God. How silly of me, he had been there when I was at the very lowest point in my life, and now thirty some years later I am there again. He never left me, I left him. After separating from my husband I decided I was going back to God, I had nothing else. My heart ached; I didn't care about anything anymore. *I had to go back to where I came from to be reminded of what I needed.* God welcomed me back in like the story of the prodigal son. He has spoken to me through his word and through Elevation Church. He has shown me things I've never seen before. I am indeed reminded even through God's Word we are always learning. Forgiveness is key in all of this. Forgiveness of our loved ones, friends, our partners, our spouse, whoever because one thing is for sure God has forgiven them. Therefore, it's in our best interest to forgive them also. If we are to truly be free and free is what we all want to be; confess to God. Don't do as David did in Psalm 32:34 (NIV), "when I kept silent my bones wasted away through my groaning all day long. For day and night, your hand was heavy on me; my strength was sapped as in the heat of summer."

One final thought as to why I believe you should never give up hope. In the summer of 2012, I went to visit one of my foster families who I had not seen in several years. Her father passed away and she had called me to let me know. I loved him dearly he was a good man, a man of God. We spent a few days together and it felt as though we hadn't missed a beat. We laughed and enjoyed the time we spent. A few months later, I went back to visit as they were moving. They purchased a larger farm a few hours away and wanted me to come check it out. So it was closing in on fall, my husband and I went to visit. It was a beautiful piece of land and I knew this was where they were supposed to be. During my visit, they ask if they could speak to me in private. My husband and other family members were outside enjoying the farm and the animals. They grabbed my hand and said we have something we want to ask you, I said okay. They said, "we would like to adopt you." You can imagine the look of surprise on my face. "Adopt me?" After all, I was thirty-five years old. I didn't need a mom and dad, right? I mean I needed a mom and dad twenty-five years before this. But not the case, I prayerfully considered this, did some adult adoption research, and found out it was a real thing. Then, I begin to realize maybe I had all I needed growing up, after all, this was the last family I lived with. What if my desire and my prayer to be adopted at an earlier age would have been answered?

Many times when we pray for things, we don't always know what we are praying for. We know what we want, but God knows what we need. I think back to the days of Moses and the Israelites, how they wandered for forty years waiting to enter the promised land. I waited twenty-five years after I entered foster care to finally have a family to call my own. A mom and dad who love me unconditionally. It indeed was worth the wait. What a blessing it has been. God is always faithful and always timely.

Printed in the USA
CPSIA information can be obtained
at www.ICGtesting.com
LVHW010741130224
771494LV00052B/176